HURLER ON THE DITCH

MICHAEL MILLS

HURLER ON THE DITCH

*Memoir of a Journalist who Became
Ireland's First Ombudsman*

CURRACH PRESS

First published in 2005 by
CURRACH PRESS
55A Spruce Avenue, Stillorgan Industrial Park, Blackrock, Co Dublin

www.currach.ie

1 3 5 4 2

Cover by Anú Design
Index by Therese Carrick
Origination by Currach Press
Printed by Betaprint Ltd, Dublin

ISBN 1-85607-919-8

Contents

For my wife, Bríd, and our children, Frances, Gerald,
Kieran, Liam, Pauline, Veronica, Michael and Stephanie.
Special thanks to Kieran for his help in preparing the manuscript.

Preface

Hurler on the Ditch was the title of a television programme which ran on RTÉ from 1963 to 1966. It was originally intended to run for three months; in fact, it ran for three-and-a-half years. The idea was sold to RTÉ management by the late writer and journalist, John Healy, who wrote a script each week about the political events of the previous week, followed by a discussion among the political correspondents of the four national daily newspapers.

The contents of this book are based on the recollections of the author from his early years until his retirement from the office of Ombudsman in 1995. It is not a historical record nor a social commentary on the times, but merely a recollection of the most vivid memories of the period as they affected me personally.

Three areas of the book are specially highlighted: the Arms Crisis which was one of the most dramatic political events of the past fifty years and which I have discussed and analysed over the past thirty years; the controversy over the border overflights which forced Jack Lynch's hand in resigning as leader and about which no other Irish journalist wrote at the time having accepted the general claim that there was no truth in the story; and finally, my fight to save the office of the Ombudsman from the financial cutbacks imposed by the Taoiseach, C. J. Haughey.

1 Early Days

One of my earliest memories is of a little boy hanging out of the second-floor window of a house overlooking the Square in Mountmellick, County Laois. A torch-lit procession was coming down the street. In front of the procession a group of men carried an effigy of the Fine Gael leader and former head of government, W. T. Cosgrave. In the middle of the Square, a bonfire blazed. As the crowds of Fianna Fáil followers cheered their approval, the effigy was hurled into the fire and sent up a cloud of sparks and smoke. The cheering went on until the speakers mounted the platform and proceeded to denounce Cosgrave and all his works. My father and mother, who were strong supporters of Fianna Fáil and Eamon de Valera, might not have objected but, even at this early age, I began to have a feeling of unease about the extent of the hatred being unleashed.

Political meetings were very often rowdy affairs with fistfights breaking out. Sometimes opponents fought one another with metal bicycle pumps hidden up their sleeves. The gardaí had to intervene to restore peace and allow the platform speaker to continue his boring address.

My father and mother were very definitely on Dev's side and actively supported the Fianna Fáil candidate, P. J. Gorry, who succeeded in getting elected to the Dáil on a number of occasions. Fine Gael had no place in our house but, strangely, a pictorial record of the lives of Arthur Griffith and Michael Collins was highly respected and was a great source of interest to

9

me and to my brothers. I can still remember the handsome features of Collins in his uniform at army parades or at hurling matches in Croke Park and then, unfortunately, his death mask following his assassination at Béal na Bláth. He remained all my life one of my great heroes.

But, Fianna Fáil was now in power and Eamon de Valera was to lead the Irish nation continuously for the next sixteen years. He was highly successful in many of his endeavours, particularly in getting back the southern ports from the British and securing our neutrality as the world hovered on the edge of another disastrous war as the 1930s came to a close. In the meantime, the Spanish civil war was in progress and we were aware of a number of young volunteers from Mountmellick going out to join the fighting. Nobody was quite sure on whose side they were fighting or if it made any difference. Anyway, we prayed and lit candles in the local church that they would be returned safely to their mothers.

The national school where my two brothers and I went was at the lower end of town. The boys were from various backgrounds, but most were poor and I recall a number of young boys in my class arriving in school in their bare feet. One boy used to wear his mother's long stockings for warmth, much to his embarrassment. The general recreation was football in the field behind the schoolhouse or handball in the newly erected alley beside the school where the Irish champion, Peter Berry, came to take part in an exhibition match on the opening day. Later in life, I was to come across the same Peter Berry as the formidable general secretary of the Department of Justice and a key witness in the Arms Trial of 1970.

My father was manager of the Mountmellick branch of the Tullamore firm of D. E. Williams having previously worked for the firm of McEvoys, where he met my mother. She came from a farming family, the Phelans, in Radestown, County Kilkenny, while he came from a remote part of northwest Mayo, known as

Gorthmelia, about two miles from Bamatra, west of Belmullet, on the road to Inver.

I had a very happy experience many years later when I brought my wife and family to visit Gorthmelia and show them the place where my father was born and reared. Close to Inver, I lost my way and was unable to decide between the many laneways and byroads running off the Inver road. Eventually I chose one exit and realised two miles later that I was completely lost and needed directions. I approached a small farmhouse to ask the lady working in the yard for directions. But, before I could speak she said, 'Don't open your mouth. I know who you are. You're a Mills.' For the first time in my life I appreciated the meaning of 'roots' and how facial characteristics of families are carried over from generation to generation.

The place where my father grew up was a small holding of about 20 acres on the edge of a common bog. It was set in the middle of dozens of similar-type holdings dotted along the hillside, where parents reared five and six children in the most difficult of circumstances. There was no electricity or telephone communication; the crop rotation was hay, oats and potatoes; the land was so poor it would not grow any other crop and it had been criss-crossed with drains and fed with lime over the years with no apparent benefit. Emigration was widespread, to England, Scotland and America. One member of a family would make it to New York or Boston, work hard and save money for a year or two until they put the fare together to bring out a brother or sister. In this way, whole families disappeared from Mayo and became citizens of the Bronx or Manhattan. As they became wealthier, they sent home food parcels and clothes, and eventually, arrived home by plane themselves every summer, hired a big car in Shannon and carried their old friends around to all the pubs in the area, much to the annoyance of wives and mothers.

The town where I grew up in Mountmellick, County Laois,

was a small one-street location with an unusually well-balanced mix of Catholics and Protestants. Many of my earliest friends were Protestant children from the main street. My mother used to say that Mountmellick was a 'little Belfast'.

My father's job as manager of D. E. Williams' stores was running into difficulty at this time and it came as no surprise to my mother when he lost his job and we had to move to another Laois town, Durrow, where my father opened a store of his own. I never had the same affection for my teachers here as in my previous schooldays but, then, I did not have the happiest of starts. One of the proudest possessions for a young fellow at the time was a catapult. Having put one together with some difficulty, I was experimenting with it one day in the garden behind our store when the young gardener asked me for the loan of it. He loaded a fair-sized stone into the sling, pulled the rubber attachment and the missile went hurtling through the air and over the rooftops. I waited in horror for the inevitable crash of glass, grabbed the catapult and ran to hide it in a shed.

The stone had crashed through head teacher Patrick Savage's window, hit the table where he was working, narrowly missed his head and struck the back wall. It was obvious from the trajectory that the shot could have come from only one source. I tried to offer a tearful explanation to my father and Mr Savage, who calmed down sufficiently to declare that he would not on this occasion inform the gardaí.

A much more serious disaster was narrowly averted shortly afterwards. The boys in my class had started to talk behind their hands about sex. Not wishing to be outdone in the general knowledge or ignorance about the subject, I made a pencil drawing of the headmaster and his wife in what can only be described as 'a compromising position'. It was a crude drawing on the side of a page of my English primer. Lest there should be any doubts about the identity of the participants in the act, I wrote the names 'Paddy' and 'Mary' underneath the figures, with

Paddy's appendage clearly sticking out in front.

The primers were collected by the headmistress from time to time to be checked. I placed mine in the middle of the bundle and blithely went home to lunch. I was halfway through my lunch when I had a sudden and shocking memory of the offending drawing. I dashed up from the table, broke all my previous sprinting records back to the school where Paddy and Mary were walking up and down on the footpath. I watched until they turned and were walking in the opposite direction, made a quick dash through the junior boys' door into the classroom, grabbed my copybook from the bundle and searched frantically in my schoolbag for an eraser. Having found it and glanced out the window to make sure that the stroll of the two teachers outside was continuing its untroubled state, I rubbed out the two pencilled figures, making sure that they could not be seen or traced underneath. Then, having deposited the book back in its place with a genuine sigh of relief and peeped out the window to make sure that Paddy and Mary were again walking in the opposite direction, I dashed out the door and joined my pals in the playground as if nothing had happened.

Meanwhile, my father was having difficulty with his new enterprise. Customers were in short supply and he was finding it hard to raise the money for the lease of the shop and house. I came home to lunch one day to find an eviction in progress. Our landlords had decided to put us out on the road for non-payment of rent. The bailiffs were putting our furniture onto the footpath, against the protests of my mother, as I arrived at the house. My father had gone in search of a council official to look for alternative accommodation and a lorry to take our belongings to our new abode. Our new house was in Ballinakill village and, a couple of hours later, we were on our way there, perched on top of the dining-room suite on the back of a hired lorry. My mother cried her fill but it was all a new adventure in our eyes. The full extent of our fall into poverty became clear only in the following months as my mother brought item after item of our belongings to the pawnbroker to raise money for food. Among the items sold was a lovely collection of books, including the full range of Charles Dickens' novels and the Waverley novels of Sir Walter Scott. They had given us a wonderful introduction to literature and I had read much of Dickens by the time I was eight years of age.

Ballinakill had many attractive features, among them a lending library located in the school, where two crates of fresh books would arrive every second week and I discovered a new hero, T. E. Lawrence, whose *Seven Pillars of Wisdom* gave me hours of enjoyment as I revelled in his remarkable adventures in the north African desert.

We had our own adventures in Heywood Estate, just outside the village, where the big house with its impressive gardens and lakes offered a rare open-air facility for the people of the village. I learned to fish for roach and perch in the lakes. My fishing rod was a bamboo shoot taken from the gardens, to which I attached a line and hook bought in the local hardware shop. Dozens of young fellows used to gather around the lakes with their home-made fishing rods in the afternoons, and march proudly down the village afterwards with their catches.

The problem of fuel for firewood was resolved for poorer families by raiding the woods around Heywood Estate. Day after day, we would trudge down the main street in Ballinakill, pulling our haul of tree branches behind us to be chopped up in the backyard.

Nine months later, we were on the move again, this time to Spink where my father had become manager of a shop and licensed premises on the road to The Swan. There, we learned for the first time how to tickle trout with our hands under the bank of a river and the skill of pulling them out with all the success of a fishing net. There, too, we learned to play cards. It was a great thrill to be asked to join the men at their midday break in the sandpit in a game of '25', to win, perhaps, ten pence and then, heartbreakingly, lose it all to my older brothers in the afternoon. No loss in playing cards or backing horses later in life ever equalled the heartbreak of losing that ten pence.

Friction arose between my father and the owner of Spink House and we were on the move again, this time to Timahoe, whose claim to fame rested on a well-preserved round tower. Cromwell had blown away the top of the tower in 1650 but it had been restored and visitors now came regularly to view the structure. It was underneath the tower that a group of local members of the Defence Forces came in the early 1940s to search for a collection of guns which somebody recalled as having been buried there in the aftermath of the civil war in the early 1920s. As it turned out, there was no collection, but only a rusted rifle which was completely useless for the purpose intended by the LDF to defend Timahoe against a contingent of German soldiers alleged to have landed near Abbeyleix by parachute that afternoon.

The first news of the invasion came by way of a telegram to the local post office saying that a German parachute had been found between Abbeyleix and Durrow. It created a certain amount of panic and the local members of the LDF, including my oldest brother, were put on the alert. It never occurred to anybody to ask how Hitler could ever have heard of Timahoe, much less why he would want to capture the place.

Anyway, preparations were made to defend our village. The members of the LDF were told to go home and get a few hours' sleep before getting up to patrol the roads after dark. The last word we had before the post office closed down for the day was that 600 Germans had landed and were even now marching on Timahoe. A terrible gloom had descended on the place, matched by low-flying clouds. Into this disturbed atmosphere came a little Morris Minor car, containing four crombie-coated middle-aged men, all wearing felt hats and with a single shotgun sticking out of one of the rear windows. They were LDF officers from Portlaoise on their way to examine the preparations being made around the county to fight the Germans.

Just then, the ominous sound of an aircraft was heard overhead. All eyes turned to the skies. As the clouds broke, the fuselage of an aircraft could be spotted in the opening. The Portlaoise officers immediately decided that it was a Luftwaffe plane, bound for the Blackhills, a small mountain range a few miles away. They decided to attempt to head it off, jumped back into their Morris Minor and set off in a cloud of dust in pursuit of the aircraft, with the shotgun protruding from the back window. The rest of us went home, more worried than ever, except my father who thought the whole thing was a major joke.

Within hours, he was proved right as word filtered through that a serious mistake had been made. The wife of a local garda officer had been out on the road, walking her dog, when she saw a cloud of what she thought were parachutists coming down out of the sky and landing in a hayfield. It transpired that what she had thought were invading German soldiers was nothing more harmful than a swarm of small cocks of hay caught in a blast of wind known locally as a 'fairy blast', hurled up into the sky and landing a hundred yards away in a neighbour's hayfield. The LDF settled back into a restful sleep, helped by the comfort of the heavy overcoat issued to all personnel when they joined the force. It provided the equivalent heat of several blankets in the cold winter nights.

Life returned to normal in Timahoe and I was up next morning to serve Fr Boland's nine o'clock Mass as usual. He was a middle-aged man, with a white head of hair, round as he was tall, who had great difficulty manoeuvring himself in and out of his little car. His slowness of movement disappeared as soon as he reached the foot of the altar and launched himself at an incredible speed into the Latin text. Over the months, I had acquired equal speed with the Latin and, no matter how fast he could travel from one prayer to the next, I could match his skill. It all became a jumble of Latin words and phrases which were unknown to anybody else except Fr Boland and myself, but, one thing was certain – the people who came to nine o'clock Mass in Timahoe were always out of the church by 9.15. The quarter-hour Mass had become a reality. Until one morning, to my dismay, Fr Boland was replaced by the parish priest from Stradbally, Fr Byrne. He started off the Mass slowly and deliberately when I hit him with a gun-burst of Latin words and phrases which left him stunned. He stopped in the middle of the prayers at the foot of the altar, looked in amazement at my bowed head and the spew of Latin pouring out of my mouth. I was already several responses ahead of him. Either he had to speed up or I had to slow down. He told me to say the responses more clearly. I was quite unable to respond to his request. As soon as he resumed the Mass, I hit him again with an outburst of Latin prayers. At this stage, he obviously decided I was a hopeless case and the Mass proceeded on the basis of a slow and deliberate enunciation of the prayers by the celebrant and a staccato burst of responses by the server. It was no fault of mine that the people did not get out of church that morning until after 9.30. Fortunately, Fr Boland was back to say Mass again the following morning and things were back to normal.

After Mass on Sunday mornings, a group of the men used to assemble on the footpath outside Kerr's corner shop to play 'pitch and toss', only that they discarded the pitching and concentrated on the tossing. A circle would form around the tosser who would throw down the stake to be covered. Each of the players would place his bet and the game was on. Nothing could interrupt the flow of the game, not even the news one Sunday morning that England had declared war on Germany. Biddy Bolton, who brought the news and who owned one of the two radios in the village was listened to with attention but her news was immediately discarded as an unnecessary interruption of the game.

Biddy Bolton had a habit of describing every day, no matter how bad the weather, as a glorious day. Old man Kerr, a Protestant shopkeeper with a massive beard, eventually declared that 'if it was raining pitchforks and Hitlers, Biddy Bolton would still say it was a glorious day'.

The central figure in the toss school was Jack Cushen, a stout small farmer who would place the two pennies on the specially cut piece of timber, toss them with a flick of the wrist into the air, say 'sound as a bell' as the coin s reached their zenith, and then watch them fall back to the ground. Two heads meant the tosser had won; two harps saw victory go to the other players; and a head and a harp meant the coins had to be tossed again.

My oldest brother won 35 shillings at the school one Sunday and went into Portlaoise the following day to buy two pairs of boots. My father made him get his money back on one pair of boots in order to buy food for the family for the rest of the week. My father was working at this time for the county council, on the roads, for thirty shillings a week, a wage which provided food for only half the week. We had to depend on Mr Kerr's credit for the rest of the week.

Physically, my father was quite incapable of doing the roadwork involved and he was lucky to find a change of job before long which paid better and made less demands. He became a travelling salesman for a British manufacturer who made corks for insertion in the mouths of beer bottles. He travelled on his bicycle around the county, calling on larger publicans with their own bottling facilities. We rented a new house a few miles away and I started school with the Patrician Brothers in Abbeyleix. The Brothers were an extraordinarily dedicated body of men who gave their lives freely and without ever asking for financial reward for their work. Indeed, when a couple of years later I moved on to Ballyfin College by way of a scholarship, I found that the Brothers were ploughing their wages back into the college so that students' fees could be maintained at £40 per annum, or less than £2 a week for board and lodging during the school year.

The Superior in Abbeyleix, Br Francis Redmond, later became Superior General of the Order and travelled all over the world to visit houses of the Order in the US, Australia, India and Africa, until he retired in later life to the monastery in Tullow, County Carlow, where I would visit him from time to time. The place has now become a golf and sports complex, known as Mount Wolseley. He was one of the best teachers I ever knew. History and Irish were his favourite subjects. I can still remember to the present day lists of dates of historical events, their causes and their effects, with great precision, just as I still find difficulty in listening to or reading commentaries in Irish without analysing and parsing the material for grammatical errors.

Another brother who later became one of my best friends was Br Denis Lomasney from Cork, who taught Maths and English and managed to convey his love for English literature and poetry to at least some of his pupils. The Superior, Br Valerian Whelan, from Wicklow, was a wonderful teacher of Latin for the decreasing number of students who were interested in the subject.

During the war years, there was a shortage of all the usual commodities of food. There was no such thing as white flour. Instead, there was a sort of light brown mixture which the brothers made up themselves and baked in their own bakery up the yard. Each of the students was limited to five half-slices per meal, with a ration of two ounces of butter and a half-pound of sugar per week. The brothers had their own farm and consequently there was a regular supply of potatoes and vegetables.

My father used to cycle the fourteen miles from home to Ballyfin regularly on Sundays to visit me, bring news from home and hear my news about events in the college. Two years after entering Ballyfin, I sat for the Intermediate Certificate and won a first-class scholarship which covered the cost of my fees for the remaining two years. About the same time, my father got ill and, after several months in hospital, died. One of the brothers drove me home in a horse and trap as there was little petrol for the driving of cars at the time.

My father's funeral to the cemetery in Abbeyleix was a lonely affair, with only the neighbours and a few of his old friends from Mountmellick in attendance. Nobody from his old political party, Fianna Fáil, attended or sent a message. The only public representative who sent a message was Independent and later Fine Gael deputy, Oliver Flanagan. My mother never lost her allegiance to Fianna Fáil but she always put Oliver Flanagan on her list afterwards.

She was now reduced to a widow's pension of twelve shillings and sixpence a week to provide for herself and my two sisters. My two brothers, who were both in the army, occasionally used to send a few shillings from their small wages. She started to keep hens, so that she always had a supply of eggs, but, at times, things got tough. I remember on one occasion digging up wild potatoes and nettles to make up a meal. The concoction was vile and we ended up laughing at the result of our cooking exercise, bearing in mind that many families across Europe were surviving on such a diet in the aftermath of the war.

I returned to school in Ballyfin to spend the remainder of the term in a sort of daze. In Ballyfin, the local parish priest was Fr O'Rourke, better known as 'Father Hat' because of the large black hat he hung inside the sacristy door and which was clearly visible to the boys going into prayers. Its presence indicated to our dismay that we were in for a lengthy sojourn in the chapel as the old priest recited various private prayers and religious poems. In my third year, he got the idea of presenting to the college a good conduct medal to be awarded to the boy who, in the eyes of the other students, represented all the best traits of young manhood. Everybody was anxious to win it, recognising at the same time the embarrassment that could be caused by carrying around this accolade for the rest of your life. The result was to be decided by popular vote, with Father Hat collecting the votes and announcing the winner on a Sunday morning in the study hall.

He made a production of the occasion. The audience of students and brothers was much larger than he would normally address and he milked it for every emotion he could create. He decided to turn the contest into a horse race, with dozens of eager students jumping over fences, many of them falling along the route. For the best part of half an hour, he had his audience involved in the imaginary steeplechase until, eventually, he tired of the sport, crashed most of the remaining contestants into the last fence and had some two or three runners coming up the straight. We waited for the winner's name. He would be a credit to the school, to his village, to his parents, and his name would be written up in the history of the school. And the boy's name was written on the back of the medal. Eventually, he stopped the nonsense and announced the winner. It was myself; I had won the first Father Hat Good Conduct medal. I lost it several times, probably deliberately, but it always turned up again until, about twenty years later, I left it behind me in digs in Drumcondra and I never saw it again. The following year, I won the Doctor Ivo Drury Trophy for all-round sports activity, a prize I valued much more highly.

That autumn, I made some extra money by working for a local farmer, thinning beet at ten pence a drill. I could thin six drills a day, which worked out at £3 for five days' work. I earned another £3 by writing an article on farming in North West Mayo for the *Farmer's Journal*. It was the first article I had accepted for publication and for which I got paid. I could afford to go to the Munster hurling final in Thurles, where I watched Mick Mackey and his brother, John, play their last game in the Limerick jersey.

As the holidays came towards an end, I started to consider my future. I had won a university scholarship on the results of the Leaving Certificate examination but I knew it would be insufficient to pay for fees and digs in the city. My mother, still with only her widow's pension, would be unable to help me. I thought of sitting for the Junior Executive examination in the civil service but I had not filled in the application form which needed to be accompanied by a £10 fee, which I did not possess. For a long time, I had been thinking vaguely about studying for the priesthood. I kept pushing the thought away but it kept recurring and I knew I could not put off a decision indefinitely.

The idea I had in mind was to join the Passionist Order, located in Mount Argus in Dublin. I had been very impressed by two priests from the Order who conducted a mission in Abbeyleix. I liked particularly the theatricality surrounding the Passionist habit, with its prominent white cross, which the missioner would take off and place on the altar before going into the pulpit to deliver his sermon. It created a very dramatic piece of action.

I told my mother about my intention and she suggested we should talk to the local curate, Fr O'Connor, who drove me to Mount Argus to talk to Fr Bonaventure a week later. The first thing the Passionist priest did was to catch my hair and pull it. 'All that hair will have to come off in the novitiate,' he said. It was a shock to me as I was very vain about my hair and the angle it should be combed. Anyway, I decided to give it a go and, within a couple of weeks, I was on my way to the Passionist novitiate at The Graan, Enniskillen.

I found myself in the company of ten other novices, eight of whom were to study to be priests and two to be brothers. We got out of bed in the mornings at two o'clock for an hour's prayer, went back to bed from three to six, and then started the day's duties, with breakfast at eight. There were two breaks during the day for recreation, which allowed us to walk in the garden if the weather was good. Otherwise, we sat in the large recreation room, reading or talking.

Each week, one of the novices would be deputed to act as prayer leader. Every half-hour or so, he would be expected to call the attention of his fellows to 'the presence of God', at which they would all stand, reply 'Jesus and Mary be praised', and sit down again. Some novices were more enthusiastic than others and would say the prayer every quarter. It was a great conversation-stopper. Somebody might be in the middle of an interesting story about his previous life in the world. When he got a chance to resume, his interest in the story might have waned, especially as God had now joined the audience.

In those early weeks, we also had to make up our disciplines, which would be used once or twice a week at early-morning prayer to whip ourselves around the buttocks. It was not a very severe punishment; you could hit yourself as hard or as lightly as you wished. Indeed, some novices got the idea of placing themselves close to the prayer stalls so that the discipline, with its rows of knotted cords, would hit the timber from time to time to create an impression of somebody giving himself a proper hiding for all his offences.

Another punishment for breaking things around the monastery, such as cups, saucers or plates, which occurred regularly during wash-up after meals, was to carry the broken plate or whatever around your neck on a piece of string and go on your knees before the rector in the dining hall, who would give you a penance, such as carrying the broken plate around for the rest of the day. It was all a big joke and nobody took it seriously. The overall discipline in the monastery was, however, a very serious matter and, as the months went by, you found yourself working on automatic. You were not permitted to make special friends, so that Br Jack and I seldom found ourselves together. He was a big northerner, over six feet tall, who had been a star footballer. He was in his early twenties, having spent some time teaching before joining the Passionists. He told me one day that he had a terrible temptation to hit the little Master of Novices over the head with a wooden sweeper. He was working away with the sweeper, minding his own business when the

Master reprimanded him for not keeping his mind on the work and being too easily distracted by every passing body. Jack lifted the sweeper as the little Master scuttled past and debated with himself whether he should bring it down on the poor man's head. If he had given in to the temptation, he would certainly have caused very serious damage and it would have been very difficult to claim provocation since one of the tasks of the Master and his assistant was to humiliate the novices with provocative remarks of this nature. The Assistant Master accused me on one occasion of trying to listen in on his conversation with another priest. Since he was one of the dullest people I had ever met, I regarded it as a serious insult.

Br Jack was blackballed in the final chapter before passing out of the novitiate and had to leave the monastery. He was determined to be a priest, however, and I met him years later as a fourth-year student in All Hallows College in Dublin, where he was ordained before going on mission work in New Zealand.

All the novices were brought to the hospital in Enniskillen for routine check-ups before going to Mount Argus for full-time studies for the priesthood. I was asked to return to see a consultant in Enniskillen. He confirmed what the X-rays had shown – that there was a shadow on one of my lungs and I would have to go into hospital for treatment. I left the Graan monastery the following week and returned home to Abbeyleix. With time on my hands, I read a great number of books and studied shorthand. One of the Patrician Brothers in Abbeyleix, Vergilius, had got a bright notion years before that shorthand would be a useful adjunct to a boy's curriculum. He ordered a batch of Pitman's shorthand manuals, and a group of us used to assemble in the school every Saturday morning for lessons in shorthand. I discovered I still had my copy of the manual, so I set down to learn the subject and develop speed in taking notes. I had nothing definite in mind; in fact, I was still thinking vaguely that I might resume my priestly studies. But, as time went by, I began to realise that my time in the monastery had turned me into something of an automaton. I began to think of taking up journalism. I now had shorthand of about 100 words a minute – not a great achievement but possibly enough to get by if I had a chance to learn how to use a typewriter.

My sister was attending the convent in Abbeyleix so I sent a note to the sister in charge, asking if I could get use of the convent's typewriters for an hour or two each week. She gave me permission and, very shortly, I had shorthand and typing of a sort. I could go looking for a job as a journalist. After all, I had written one or two very naive short stories, and an article for the *Farmer's Journal*, had reviewed a couple of entirely forgettable books and could turn out shorthand at about 100 words a minute.

I watched the advertisements in the newspapers and, one day, there was an advertisement looking for a senior reporter on a provincial paper in Bray, County Wicklow. I applied for the job and was quite surprised to get a letter from the editor asking me to call him on the phone the following day. He told me I did not have enough experience for the Bray job but the company, which ran four different papers from Wexford, would like me to join the staff as a junior reporter. They would train me. I jumped at the offer and started work in Wexford town at £4 a week.

My first assignment was to write an obituary of a local lady who had died in Bride Street. I called to the house to collect the details. Her sister gave me all the facts and proceeded to give me the names of all the relatives, down to the cousins. At that stage, I tried to call a halt and suggested that we did not really need to list all the cousins. She looked at me quite coldly and said, '*The Free Press* [a rival paper] took the cousins and you'll take the cousins,' I took the cousins but they never appeared in print.

I found the People Newspapers a happy place to work. I had a good tutor in the senior reporter, Eddie O'Keefe, who covered all the main stories, attended all the courts and council meetings and contributed the bulk of the material in the paper every week.

He wore a peaked cap at all times, indoors and outdoors, and at weekends he would disappear into the country to shoot birds, wearing his rubber wellies. That night, he would find a dance somewhere in the locality and dance the night away, still wearing his wellington boots.

The paper had one rule about court cases — there was to be no reporting of cases of a sexual nature. To judge from the various rumours in circulation in the town, Wexford had its fair share of sexual abuse, but it was not something that was talked about except in whispers. It would be many years before clerical sex abuse hit the headlines. After a couple of months in Wexford, I was sent to Wicklow to take the place of a senior reporter who had become ill. I spent the next six months in Wicklow, barely keeping my head above water as I struggled to cover courts and council meetings during the day and tried to translate my shorthand notes into English at night, on an old and well-worn typewriter. Next morning, I would put the finished product on an early train to Wexford.

I was forced to learn all the requirements for a senior journalist during my period in Wicklow. Events which I would not have been allowed to report on without years of experience became a daily routine. I would spend long hours in the day at sittings of the High Court circuit. I got to know a great deal about the pomp of the judicial system and the arrogance of many of the judges.

I was to witness the same arrogance many years later among some of my colleagues in the Ombudsman profession, where Ombudsmen held the same status as High Court judges. At a conference of Ombudsmen in Helsinki, a number of Asian delegates became so irritated by the prima donna behaviour of some of the European delegates that a senior Ombudsman from Sri Lanka, who had been a former judge of the Supreme Court, decided to make a point of it. He suggested that an Ombudsman's first task each morning after getting out of bed should be to go down on his knees and pray for humility. A few of us applauded the sentiment but most of the delegates regarded it as insensitive and unjustifiable.

The inability of most people to handle positions of authority without becoming insensitive and offensive became a source of great curiosity to me, particularly in regard to politicians in later years, although I was to see the earliest examples of it in the newspaper world. After six months in Wicklow, I transferred to Bray, where I was to spend four happy years. The demands on reporting for the *Wicklow People* were not very onerous and I had a great deal of free time which I spent with my friends at Bray Cove Swimming Club, allegedly watching out for items of news but, in reality, talking about sporting events, analysing the latest books and films and making plans to see new plays in Dublin.

One of the great attractions of Bray was its proximity to Dublin, which enabled me to develop my interest in theatre with regular visits to the Abbey, located at the time in the old Queen's in Pearse Street, the Gaiety and the Gate. I also had the benefit of the annual visit to Bray for several months each summer of the Brendan Smyth Academy of actors who brought a good selection of European drama as well as some of the best Irish plays by O'Casey, Synge, Lennox Robinson and Louis D'Alton. I became good friends with many of the actors, notably Vincent Dowling, later of the Abbey Theatre, Claire Mullan and her actor-husband, Conor Evans, Beryl Fagan, wife of Brendan Smyth, Laurie Morton, Norman Rodway and Pauline Delaney – friendships which were renewed when I moved into Dublin later to join the staff of *The Irish Press*.

The Irish Press I discovered to be a quite uneasy place. Labour relations were at a very bad point and showed little improvement over the years until the place closed down eventually some years after I left. Working conditions were quite poor. The newsroom, where some thirty reporters worked, was grossly overcrowded. Chairs were in such short supply that one reporter, in desperation, wrote his name on the seat of a chair and tied the chair to the leg of a table with a piece of rope. There was some improvement when new offices were opened up and the entire production team moved into one huge room, like the image of *The Washington Post* later portrayed in the film on Watergate.

The newsroom was immediately inside the door with the News Editor and his assistants sitting at the top table. They lived in constant fear of visits or telephone calls from the Managing Director, Vivion de Valera, who operated from an office across in O'Connell Street, and who made constant forays to Burgh Quay, where, as he told a group of trade unionists on one occasion, he believed in running the organisation with an iron hand. That spirit transmitted itself down the line to the rest of the staff.

It took many years of struggle and outright confrontation to break down that spirit. In the meantime, some of the best staff had left to work in *The Irish Times* or the *Independent*, men like Niall Carroll, Arthur Noonan and Des Rushe who could no longer accept the spirit of intimidation that prevailed in the *Press*.

Many of the best journalists in Ireland passed through the doors of the *Press*. Famous names like Maurice Liston, Terry Ward, Ben Kiely, Sean J. White, Pádraig Puirséal and Séamus de Faoite were to be met there on a daily basis and to contribute to the feeling of awe that a young man like myself brought to the scene.

Maurice Liston, a big-hearted republican from Limerick, whose knowledge of agricultural matters was phenomenal but whose talents were largely wasted by lower-grade markings such as covering the district courts or monthly meetings of county committees of agriculture, was asked on one occasion to check out a report of a fire in a convent down the country. Some time later, the News Editor asked him if there was anything in the story. 'No,' Maurice replied in his rich Limerick accent. 'I was talking to the Reverend Mother herself and she told me there was fuck all in it.' Maurice was a legend who did more to promote goodwill for *The Irish Press* than all the public relations officers employed by the management. On one occasion, he was suspended for three days for a silly mistake which should not have required even a rebuke, never mind a humiliating suspension. Nobody in management in *The Irish Press* ever sat down to consider what was happening to the place or to appreciate the level of hostility that was being created between management and staff.

The sports sub-editors occupied a series of desks next to the newsroom. Here, Paddy Purcell wrote daily about GAA matters and, in his spare time, researched material for a massive history of the GAA on which he had been working for a number of years. While still a student at UCD, he wrote a couple of good novels which suggested he might become a best-selling novelist but a disappointment with one publication which narrowly failed to make first choice of the American Book Club set him back and, when it was followed by a rebuff from Hollywood over a short story, 'The Quiet Man', he lost heart. Some backroom employee in Los Angeles found that his film company had already taken an option on another author's 'The Quiet Man', which was subsequently turned into the John Wayne–Maureen O'Hara classic. Paddy and I used to travel home from the office many nights about midnight. I would drop him off in Harold's Cross and continue to Templeogue.

Shortly after joining *The Irish Press*, I became ill and had to go into hospital. For more than a year, Maurice Liston visited me every Sunday with the proceeds of a small collection he made from the reporting staff to enable me to buy essential items. The generosity of this big-hearted man was quite overwhelming. A spirit of camaraderie prevailed among the staff which even the bad vibes from management could not kill. This was despite the motley nature of many of the staff. The news sub-editors' desk, for example, had among its staff two former Chiefs of Staff of the IRA, several young barristers who were holding themselves in waiting for big jobs down in the Four Courts, a middle-aged man who was attached to a militant Catholic organisation and who regularly produced his rosary beads to say his prayers during lulls in the workload, and an eccentric poet who used to carry his bicycle up the stairs and turn it upside down in the middle of the room to carry out necessary repairs.

I did the work of a general reporter and occasionally sat in on the desk to assist the news editor. I was offered the job of film critic which I accepted with enthusiasm, not only because I loved cinema but because it paid an extra £3 a week. I had just got married and an additional £3 a week was a big help. The disadvantage was that I had to give up my free day each week to attend the cinema. I made the mistake of trying to cover all the new films each week and, since there was usually a change of feature in five or six of the cinemas, I would finish my viewing about nine or ten o'clock each Friday, having commenced viewing about two o'clock. I would then go home and try to unravel the maze of plots and documents at my typewriter, in order to have my copy in the office next morning. It was an impossible undertaking and when, some years later, I left the position, my successor, Séamus de Faoite, wisely confined himself to one or two reviews a week.

One of the most peculiar features of *The Irish Press* was that, despite its constant and unthinking support of the Fianna Fáil party, nobody on the staff was ever asked to declare his or her politics. Most of the staff had no political allegiance. Some who felt an attachment to Fianna Fáil became cynical as the years went by and they witnessed considerable hypocrisy in relation to so-called national causes, such as the revival of the Irish language and reunification of the country. Many of the employees would have a natural attraction for the Labour Party because of their trade union activities. There were several socialists and there was even a Trotskyite for a short time.

Whatever your allegiance, you knew that certain politicians were lower class and had to be treated accordingly. Eamon de

Valera was sacred. Every utterance, no matter how banal, had to be reported. Special reporters were assigned to cover his speeches and to travel with him wherever he went, especially during election campaigns. They were the top shorthand note-takers who would visit Dev's hotel room each morning, take notes of the speech he intended to make that evening, and then check their notes against delivery.

There could be no short-cuts with his speeches. They had to be reported verbatim. The speeches of members of Fine Gael and Labour were treated almost with contempt, the general idea being that they should know their place. That place was not very high in the priority of news in *The Irish Press*. I remember one occasion when George Douglas, who was acting political correspondent at the time, became excited about a speech by Pat Lindsay, a very clever barrister and possibly the finest raconteur I ever met. He and I became good friends. On this occasion, he was delivering an attack on government policy on education, in a speech which Douglas thought was worthy of more than the usual cursory paragraph. He was quickly disillusioned of any such notion by the little editor, Frank Carty, who told him that Mr Lindsay was entitled to express his opinion of the government 'briefly'.

During election campaigns, reporters were detailed to follow leading Fine Gael and Labour spokesmen around the country, not for the purpose of reporting their speeches but to see if they would say anything derogatory about one another's party which might be used to undermine any suggestion of a coalition between them after the election. I was assigned to cover P. J. Crotty, of Kilkenny, who had been a junior Fine Gael minister in a previous coalition. He kindly offered me a lift in his car from Kilkenny out to Callan where he was holding one of his rallies. I rang my news desk towards the end of the rally to report that I had heard nothing that could remotely be described as an attack on the Labour Party. I omitted to tell the news editor, of course, that I was standing sufficiently far way from the platform that I could not hear a word the speaker was saying. In view of the fact that I was expecting a lift back to Kilkenny from the speaker, I was hardly going to be so underhanded as to report any embarrassing utterances he might make.

Other reporters were not so fortunate in their choice of speaker. Aidan Hennigan, afterwards London editor of the *Press* for many years, was assigned to cover the Fine Gael leader, James Dillon. He was the finest orator of his time, a delight to listen to whether in the Dáil or in a public square, unless, like Hennigan, who was clearly identifiable by his white hair, you were picked out by the speaker as the 'representative of *Pravda*' who was not attending the meeting for any good cause. In that situation, all you could do was to beat a hasty retreat.

The thinking involved in this exercise was as futile as it was stupid but, then, it was not very surprising when you contemplated the sheer stupidity of most of *The Irish Press* editorials of the time. They were based on the belief that everything that Fianna Fáil did was right and everything that Fine Gael did was wrong. It was a childish game of cowboys and Indians, except that the players were adults. It was losing the paper thousands of readers. The older generation of readers was diminishing and was not being replaced. The management of the paper could not recognise the changes taking place in Irish society and went blithely along the way thinking a change of editor was all that was required. It was only when the circulation figures could no longer be ignored that the management realised something drastic was required.

It is not possible, without great difficulty, to alter a pattern and a tradition built up over many years, without stepping on many sensitive toes. Many members of staff who were involved in the process of change had been there for many years. They had grown up with a system where even the word 'sex' was suspect. I tried to write a review of a second-rate British farce on one occasion but could not get around a central idea in the plot that one of the characters had a sex change. Eventually, I hit on a formula which passed the censorious attention of a senior sub-editor by suggesting that one of the characters had gone to America for an operation and had come back 'a changed person'. On another occasion, I was asked to discuss with the director of Dublin Zoo a series of photographs and attached scripts which he had collected on a tour of safari parks in Africa. His photos of a rhinoceros were accompanied by a script suggesting that the horn of the rhinoceros when ground into a powder was much in demand as an aphrodisiac. I wondered what the older hands in the *Press* would make of that description. Eventually, it appeared with a small amendment that the horn of the rhino was much in demand 'for medicinal purposes'.

I had become drama critic of *The Irish Press* in the mid-1950s, almost by default, after Niall Carroll, brother of dramatist, Paul Vincent Carroll, who had been drama critic for a number of years, left to join the *Independent*. He and I had become good friends and used to attend race meetings every weekend in and around Dublin, where we would occasionally meet poet Paddy Kavanagh, whom Niall regarded as 'a bit of an old cod' although he had a great affection for his poetry. He used to recite with great relish at parties 'My soul was an old horse'. I tried to convince him that the sentiments in the poem were phoney but he refused to listen to my opinion until in later life, Kavanagh himself admitted that the poem was faulty.

The payment for covering an opening night at the theatre was one guinea but I had such a love for the theatre that the fee was of secondary importance. I could now get to see and comment on all the new plays, and I loved it. It was only later when I set down my costs against the fee that I realised I was actually paying *The Irish Press* for allowing me to review drama. I raised the matter with the editor who assured me he would look into the matter, after first reminding me that I was getting into the shows free. He came back to me a week later with the 'good news' that the fee had been increased to a guinea and a half.

It was not the most adventurous period in Irish theatre but it had many exciting developments such as the formation of the Globe Theatre, operating from the Gas Company premises in Dún Laoghaire, and Phyllis Ryan's productions at the newly opened Eblana Theatre in Busáras. There was also the arrival on the scene of a brilliant young writer from Tuam, Tom Murphy, whose realistic *A Whistle in the Dark* set the stage alight. Hugh Leonard's *Madigan's Lock* was one of many clever plays from the Killiney writer and Brian Friel's *Philadelphia, Here I Come* proved that a successful short-story writer could make the transition to the stage with startling originality. It was a great privilege to come out of these productions and have the opportunity to urge people in the street to get in and see the rise of these new stars.

I started to ring Sean O'Casey occasionally at his Torquay home. My objective in calling him was to try to persuade him to lift the ban he had imposed on all productions of his plays in Dublin, following the refusal of the Archbishop of Dublin, Dr John Charles McQuaid, to allow a votive Mass to be said for the opening of the Tóstal festival. O'Casey had written a play specially for the festival called *The Drums of Father Ned*. It was a light-hearted piece of nonsense which poked fun at much of the pomposity in the church and was unlikely to give offence to anybody. The archbishop's decision gave it huge publicity and drew attention to O'Casey's earlier conflicts with church authorities and his occasional interest in Communist Russia.

At first, he refused to talk to me unless I spoke in Irish. I explained to him that I had not spoken Irish for more than thirty years and would find it very difficult to carry on a conversation, particularly over the phone. He told me that I should be ashamed of myself but, anyway, he would talk to me in English.

Once the ice was broken, I found him to a very affable character with an insatiable curiosity about Dublin and the state of drama in the city. I named for him all the new playwrights, many of whose work he already knew. When I praised one particular writer, he immediately interrupted to tell that he wasn't 'worth a curse. He's a one-play author; he will never be heard of again.' His prediction turned out to be exactly right.

I talked to him about Brendan Behan for whose writing he had some respect, but he warned, 'He will kill himself. He has no discipline.' He went on to speak of the need for a writer to exercise discipline if he wanted to succeed. It was a lonely life but it had its own rewards.

O'Casey wanted to know the names of all the drama critics attached to the Dublin papers. I told him their names and he wanted to know why we did not put our names to the bottom of the review, but only our initials. I told him it was a tradition that had grown up. He exploded – 'Tradition be damned. O'Casey was never afraid to put his name to anything he wrote. Why should you be afraid?'

Eventually, we got around to the real reason why I had called him – the ban on his plays.

'But,' he said, 'it was your bloody archbishop who banned my play.'

I asked him to be fair-minded. The archbishop had not banned his play. He had simply refused to allow a votive Mass to be said for the opening to the festival.

'That may be,' he replied, 'but the craw thumpers ran away. O'Casey is not going to run away.'

I said I would not expect him to run away but to consider the many thousands of young people who would be deprived of seeing such masterpieces as *Juno and the Paycock* or *The Shadow of a Gunman* if he persisted with his ban. 'Anyway,' I said, 'I know you are a decent man and that you will consider the case I am making to you.'

'Indeed,' he replied, 'I am not a decent man but I will think about what you have been saying.'

We agreed that I would ring him again in a month's time to see if anything had changed. Nothing changed and, over a period time, I realised that my arguments were having little effect. It was a long time before he lifted the ban and only after several people had gone to Torquay to talk to him personally.

2 Introduction to Politics

My first introduction to Leinster House was about 1957 when I was assigned with two other reporters to cover Dáil debates. I was unfortunate that the debate on that occasion was about Northern Ireland and that my job involved reporting the speech of Eamon de Valera. I spent half an hour noting down his words and then handed over to my colleague to continue the task. In transcribing my notes, I found what I thought was an obvious contradiction in Dev's speech. I removed the contradiction, replacing it with what I thought he intended to say, and carried on.

When I returned to the office that night, I was met by a trio of very disturbed people, led by the managing director, Major Vivion de Valera, who wanted to know if I had lost my reason in attempting to rewrite a speech by the great man. I explained to them my difficulty in reporting an obvious contradiction in the speech. They explained to me that Mr de Valera did not contradict himself and that anything he said must be reported exactly as he said it. In the end, the major conceded that, apart from this faux pas, my report was reasonably good. There the matter ended, but I was very happy not to be sent back to Leinster House for seven years afterwards. I went back eventually as political correspondent on a trial period for six months and remained for twenty years. My appointment came about in strange circumstances.

The position of political correspondent of *The Irish Press* had been vacant for a long time and was filled on a temporary basis by a variety of people. Nobody really wanted a job that was seen by a journalist as a propagandist operation. As has been mentioned, the approach was based on the belief that everything Fianna Fáil did was good and everything Fine Gael or Labour did was bad. It was a most stupid approach to politics and no self-respecting journalist wanted to be associated with it.

Seán Lemass, who succeeded de Valera as leader, was an outstanding politician, possibly the best leader the country ever had. He led an extremely good minority government into the early 1960s, depending on the support of a motley group of Independents, none of whom wanted to risk the loss of his seat in a new election. The Government, being short of money, decided to introduce a new tax to be known as turnover tax, which was the precursor of VAT. There were considerable doubts as to whether the Independents would continue to support the Government on this unpopular measure which was going to increase the price of food, clothes and footwear.

I was asked to go to the Dáil to do an advance piece on the possible outcome of the vote on this new tax. Having spent six years at this time studying and analysing stage productions in the theatre, it seemed fairly easy to me to anticipate what people like Joe Sheridan, Jim Carroll and Jim Sherwin were likely to do. All three made speeches containing general criticism of the new tax, but without indicating their voting intentions. I concluded that they were only putting on a show for their supporters and had no intention whatever of voting against the Government proposal.

I wrote a story on these lines for *The Irish Press* and was surprised to find that my colleagues in the other morning papers had taken the opposite view. They thought the overthrow of the Government was imminent. In fact, some government ministers took a similar view and started clearing out their desks. In the event, however, the Independents voted with the Government and the turnover tax became a reality.

Major de Valera was quite impressed with my performance

and suggested to me that I should become political correspondent. I indicated that I was not really interested in the role. He pressed me and eventually I agreed to do the job on a trial basis for six months, on condition that I would not be required to write propaganda of any description. He agreed and an uneasy relationship developed between the two of us, which over the years turned eventually into a kind of friendship, as his view of life and of politics mellowed.

The three most interesting politicians in Leinster House at the time were Charles J. Haughey, Donogh O'Malley and Brian Lenihan. Haughey was the leader of the group but O'Malley was the driving force. Lenihan was a lesser figure but hugely important in the context of the group's ambitions to win the leadership of Fianna Fáil for Haughey whenever Lemass decided to step down.

After a short but highly successful seven years in office, Lemass caught everybody by surprise by deciding to resign. One afternoon, I got a tip-off of his intention from one of his friends, who, I believe, was asked by him to pass on the information to me. The editor, Joe Walsh, raised some doubt about the accuracy of the story, which was understandable since he did not know the source and he had to rely on my assurance that the source was impeccable. We ran the story as a lead item on the front page of *The Irish Press* the following morning. It was followed by denials from all quarters, including the government information service. This led to my story being rubbished in the other papers over the next couple of days. The editor began to get worried as the weekend approached and there was no confirmation. I assured him that the story was true and there would be confirmation, but he said we would have to start a pull back unless there was some support for the story that evening. He asked me to begin preparing a withdrawal story for the Saturday paper. I asked him to hang on until six o'clock. Just a quarter of an hour before six, a messenger arrived with a statement that Mr Lemass had summoned a special meeting of the Fianna Fáil Parliamentary Party for the following Monday morning.

There was great activity over the weekend. George Colley, who was on his way to a meeting of the World Bank in the US, was advised by Lemass to return home. He was likely to be one of the contenders for the leadership. The other main contender was Haughey, whose campaign was headed by O'Malley. Jim Gibbons, a Kilkenny deputy, who was later to become Minister for Defence, was Colley's campaign manager. The newspapers were neutral in their coverage of the campaign, apart from *The Irish Times* where John Healy went overboard for Haughey, an attachment which was to last for the remainder of Healy's life. He became completely propagandist in his support of Haughey and poured scorn on the pretensions of Colley.

Healy had arrived in Dublin from Charlestown in Mayo with an extraordinarily energetic approach to journalism. His output was prodigious. He could write about politics, rural drama, fishing and pop music with equal facility, and very often he could write very well. Two books he wrote about life in the west of Ireland, *Nobody Shouted Stop* and *Nineteen Acres*, will survive as chronicles of the social and economic history of the west in the 1950s. He was a formidable supporter of the Haughey camp, and he and O'Malley became extremely close. At the time, Healy was writing the best weekly column on politics, in *The Irish Times* every Saturday. It contained considerable information about meetings of the Government which were supposed to be entirely confidential, but aspects of which O'Malley leaked to Healy. Lemass became so worried about the leaks at one stage that he warned the cabinet that, if he found the culprit, he would sack him immediately. I think he suspected O'Malley but was too fond of him to take any action.

O'Malley was one of the most charming people I ever met. He was witty and urbane and a wonderful companion. He loved the company of journalists and they, in turn, delighted in listening to his many stories about life in Limerick in his student days. Some of the stories I heard on different occasions but he never repeated them in the same context. He added details to meet the occasion or to heighten the drama. At the same time, there was a great innocence about much of his behaviour. He asked a group of us to visit his apartment in Donnybrook for a party where the main and only course was strawberries and cream. He bought in several punnets of strawberries and two-pound bags of sugar, accompanied by cartons of rich cream. Arthur Noonan, the political correspondent of the *Irish Independent*, had a bad stomach and kept resisting O'Malley's attempts to give him extra helpings. 'Get them into you, Arthur,' he kept urging a reluctant Noonan until all the strawberries had been eaten and we then sat around to discuss various ideas put forward by O'Malley for social and economic development.

He was a fund of ideas. Lemass told me that he would often come into his office with a series of proposals, most of which could be discarded quickly, but then there would be one or two gems well worth pursuing. He was lonely in his apartment and would frequently ring Healy late at night to join him for cup of tea and a chat about what 'we are going to write about' in the column on Saturday. He was very much a realist and realised long before Healy and others that the tide was running against Haughey in the succession race. Deputies were not enthusiastic about Colley but they preferred him to Haughey, whom they did not trust at all.

There were aspects of Haughey's character which worried many people. He was seen as arrogant and overambitious. To balance these defects, he was clearly the brightest politician in the Dáil, with a masterly understanding of his brief in every department he headed. I remember one day in the Dáil being very impressed by his performance as Minister for Finance. The Fine Gael leader, James Dillon, stopped me in the corridor to ask me about Haughey's speech. I told him it was a very impressive performance. Dillon agreed, but then issued a very strange warning. 'Don't ever get too close to that man,' he said. 'There is a fatal flaw in his character, which will manifest itself sooner or later and people around him will be badly hurt.' I carried the warning around with me for years afterwards but I had already decided that I did not want to make any commitment to Haughey. He wanted total commitment. He was not interested in objectivity.

A development during the succession race for the leadership gave special cause for concern. I had a call from George Colley one Sunday evening, asking me to meet him at his house. I drove down to his place to learn that the reason he could not talk to me on the phone was that he had been advised that his phone was tapped. He thought it was likely that my phone was also tapped. It was the first indication I had of a sinister element in Haughey's campaign. The irony was that he was eventually to lose the office of Taoiseach and leader of Fianna Fáil thirty years later following his involvement in the tapping of two journalists' phones.

A few days later, I had a phone call from Kevin Boland to say that he was nominating Neil Blaney for the leadership. Blaney, like Boland, did not trust Haughey, but neither liked the idea of Colley's being leader. I wrote the story for the *Evening Press* and, almost immediately, Lemass called Jack Lynch to his office to try to persuade him again to run for the office. Lynch eventually agreed to allow his name to go forward.

Blaney and Haughey withdrew their names but Colley decided to let his name stand. In the subsequent election, he was defeated by Lynch by 56 votes to 19. Lynch went on to become the most popular leader in modern Irish history and, in his first general election, three years later, became the first leader in more than twenty years to secure an overall majority for Fianna Fáil. It was a campaign in which visits to convents all over Ireland became a feature. Lynch was at his most charming and utterly convincing. I formed a liking for him at that time which remained strong all through the remainder of his political life.

All this time, my colleagues and I were appearing regularly on television in a show called *The Hurler on the Ditch*. It arose from an idea sold to RTÉ by John Healy who proposed to write a weekly script analysing political events for the previous week, which would serve as a base on which a general discussion would take place among the political correspondents for the national dailies.

Arthur Noonan represented the *Irish Independent*, Michael McInerney *The Irish Times*, John O'Sullivan the *Cork Examiner* and I represented *The Irish Press*. Healy was to act as chairman of the discussion. The intention was that the show would run for a trial period of three months; in fact, it ran for three-and-a-half years. In that time, all of us became known nationally and were regularly stopped in the street by passers-by to sign autographs. This became a matter of some concern to members of the Dáil who watched in dismay as the attention of visitors to Leinster House switched from the members to a group of lowly journalists who were not at all anxious for notoriety. Michael McInerney and I got a bit of a letdown one evening as we were walking down D'Olier Street to our offices. There was a crossing for pedestrians at the bottom of the street and, just as we approached the lights where a substantial queue had formed to cross the street, a little porter hopped out of his box inside the door of the old Ballast Office. He put up his hand to stop McInerney and myself. We awaited the usual compliment and tried to think of something suitably humble to reply when he said at the top of his voice, so that all the waiting pedestrians would hear, 'Yez know fuck-all about it.' The audience collapsed in laughter, while Michael and I tried to cover our embarrassment.

We were aware that audience response to the show was very good but we had a problem. Our chairman was extremely poor. He could turn out thousands of words on a typewriter with little difficulty, but when he was placed before a microphone, he stuttered and had great difficulty in expressing his thoughts. When a lull occurred in the discussion, he was quite incapable of picking it up and turning the discussion on to a new topic. Fortunately for the programme, Brian Farrell was called in to take over the chair, and a more professional programme emerged.

After the show had run for almost two years, we had a chat about the fee we were being paid. While we were delighted to have an extra £12 in our pockets every week, we knew that our fees were well below what others were getting in RTÉ. We decided to look for an increase, and Michael McInerney and I were delegated to do the negotiation. Michael, who had spent most of his life as a trade unionist negotiating with newspaper proprietors for sums from 5 shillings to £1, was quite incapable of pressing seriously for money which he felt we had not really earned. When I suggested to him before going into the meeting that we should look for a fee of £20, he thought it was highly immoral. I suggested to him that he should remain silent and I would make the case. The man in charge of negotiations for RTÉ was Jack White, a very talented man who had previously worked for *The Irish Times* and had written some good novels, such as *One for the Road* and *The Hard Man*. He immediately turned down our claim for £20 but the fact that he was not surprised or shocked by it led me to press for £18 as the bottom line. He accepted, and our fees were increased by 50 per cent. We could now afford steak every day.

I had known from the start that my appearance on the programme would not find favour with Fianna Fáil activists. They expected the political correspondent of *The Irish Press* to promote the Fianna Fáil line and were quite angry that I was trying to present an independent line. I had started by pushing the boat out from the shore little by little, in the hope that before long I would be sufficiently far out from the shore that they could not do anything about it. Branches of the party started passing resolutions calling for my dismissal by *The Irish Press*, and when the regional branch of the party in Mayo passed a similar resolution, I knew that Major Vivion would be worried.

He told me that he was having a lot of trouble with objectors. I said that I was aware of some of the objections but he told me I did not know the half of it. 'But,' he said, 'do not let it worry you. I trust you and I will stand by you.' I expressed my thanks for his support, which was very brave in the circumstances. The show continued until, after three-and-a-half years, RTÉ decided that it would be a better programme if it included politicians. I argued against the change on the grounds that politicians would follow a party line, there would be no independent voice and the audience would lose interest very quickly. The management in RTÉ, however, had made the decision, and *The Hurler on the Ditch* was brought to an end.

Fortunately, a very good current affairs programme, *Seven Days*, emerged in time from the reshaping of programmes, and RTÉ established a first-class investigative team, which produced many impressive programmes. RTÉ became the first group to run regular opinion polls on the state of the parties. These polls provided a very reliable guide to trends in voting patterns which became apparent at election times, and the newspapers were forced to adopt a similar approach in later years.

In 1969, however, when Jack Lynch fought his first general election as leader of Fianna Fáil, opinion polls were untested and parties could gauge possible support only by the response of the public in door-to-door canvassing or the attendance at election rallies around the country. In this regard, Lynch scored heavily, attracting large crowds for evening meetings in the squares of the larger towns and gaining more confidence in his presentation with every meeting.

It was also the first time that any party leader decided to test the strength of the religious vote, by visiting convents all over the country. It was an extraordinary development in the method of fighting elections and it was highly successful. It was not an exercise that could be repeated and, wisely, it was not adopted again.

On this occasion, it worked so well that Fianna Fáil was returned to power with an overall majority, an achievement that had not been realised by Sean Lemass in two elections earlier in the decade. The success strengthened Lynch's authority over the party but it did not lessen the ambitions of Haughey's supporters to replace this 'caretaker' Taoiseach before long. Haughey was still the dominant figure in government and, indeed, many deputations coming to Government Buildings were more interested in meeting with Haughey than with Lynch. Haughey was decisive and quick-thinking. He impressed all who met him with the clarity of his thinking and his ability to get to the root of a problem.

He suffered a great loss with the premature death of his good friend, Donogh O'Malley, who collapsed during a by-election campaign one Sunday afternoon, to the great regret of his many friends. I cried when I heard the news. I had grown extremely fond of his ebullient character, and valued the warmth of his friendship, and his liberal thinking on so many issues, which was not governed by consideration of tradition or party outlook. He had asked me to call up to his room in Leinster House two days earlier for a chat. He had undergone extensive tests at the Mater Hospital some days earlier and had been told there was no evidence of any serious ailment, but it was obvious he was not fully assured. I was anxious to get back to my work but he kept urging me to sit and talk. He was obviously lonely and worried, but as usual he made jokes and told stories. His death on the following Sunday was a great loss to his host of friends, and especially to the Fianna Fáil party which could ill afford to lose a courageous and original thinker.

The person who missed him most was Haughey. With his departure, Haughey lost a very valuable source of advice. Had

O'Malley been around, it is possible that Haughey would never have become involved in the Arms Crisis of 1970 which rocked the nation and threatened to split the Fianna Fáil party.

3 The Arms Crisis

When the Arms Crisis began in 1969, Jack Lynch had been Taoiseach for three years. He had no ambition to be Taoiseach and had only reluctantly allowed his name to be put forward after some persuasion by Seán Lemass. He faced George Colley, who was reluctant to withdraw, despite urgings from Lemass. Colley said that he would have to go home and consult with his wife on the matter, which led to Lemass remarking to one of his colleagues rather tetchily that he was saddled with a right group of ministers − one going home to consult with his wife as to whether he should allow his name to go forward and the other going home to consult with his wife as to whether he should withdraw.

There was little doubt among observers that George Colley would win a contest with Haughey. Donogh O'Malley had already advised Haughey that he was likely to be defeated when Kevin Boland nominated Neil Blaney for the post. It was at this stage that Lemass, fearing a dangerous split in the party, called in Lynch, who had earlier indicated that he did not wish to be considered, and asked him to reconsider his position in the interests of party unity. Jack Lynch decided to stand, Charlie Haughey and Neil Blaney withdrew their names, leaving only George Colley in the contest. Lynch became what many people saw as a reluctant leader. Ironically, George Colley, who allowed his name to stand in the leadership contest, was the only one of the contenders who remained constantly loyal to Jack Lynch in the succeeding years.

Lynch's control over the party remained very much in doubt until the Arms Crisis in 1969, despite his winning an overall majority in the general election of that year. A challenge to his authority arose immediately after the election when he attempted to move Neil Blaney from his job as Minister for the Environment to a new post. Blaney resisted the move and Jack Lynch did not insist. Lynch's failure to assert his authority on this occasion was bound to lead to further trouble down the line, especially as unrest began to be manifested in Northern Ireland, with civil rights protests being opposed by unionist mobs.

Blaney threw down the challenge with a speech in County Donegal suggesting that de Valera, in founding Fianna Fáil, had never ruled out the possibility of force being used to end partition, provided that force came from within the six counties. Lynch's rebuttal of Blaney's claim was weak. He said publicly that he had spoken to Blaney and rebuked him for his Donegal speech, but Blaney claimed that the rebuke consisted of a chat on the stairs of Leinster House as they were both ascending the steps to enter the Dáil chamber.

In any case, the rebuke was ineffective and, shortly afterwards, Blaney expressed exactly the same sentiments at a meeting in Kerry.

The public perception of Jack Lynch at this time was of a 'caretaker' Taoiseach, with a number of people waiting their chances to take over. In the forefront was Charlie Haughey, who as Minster for Finance controlled the most important area of government and appeared to act independently of his cabinet colleagues. Many people in Fianna Fáil felt, indeed, that Haughey was, effectively, running the country. There were signs, however, that he may have been worried by Neil Blaney's seizing the republican ground with his speeches in Donegal and Kerry.

While most observers did not give Neil Blaney much hope of success in a contest with George Colley and Charlie Haughey for the leadership in 1966, Neil Blaney himself had no such doubts. He claimed to have been surprised by the extent of the backing he received in the party after Kevin Boland proposed him, and indicated to me that he would be a very serious contender when a vacancy arose again.

That vacancy was mistakenly believed to be imminent when Jack Lynch became ill while attending a function in Ballinasloe in mid-1969. The rumour was that he had suffered a heart attack when, in fact, all that had occurred was that he got weak after smoking a pipe of tobacco that disagreed with him. He was sitting down to dinner when he reached into his pocket for his pipe and tobacco pouch. Unfortunately, he had left the pouch behind him in his state car. While his driver went to fetch the missing pouch, the Archbishop of Tuam, who was sitting beside Mr Lynch, offered him a pipeful of tobacco from his own pouch. After taking a couple of puffs, Mr Lynch complained of feeling unwell and was forced to leave table. He recovered quickly once he was assisted out to the fresh air.

The story did not suffer in the telling in the following weeks, with the result that it was generally believed that Lynch would soon step down from the leadership. The succession stakes were in full swing again, with Haughey and Blaney regarded as the frontrunners. For some strange reason, George Colley was not seen as a prominent contender. If the contest was to be between Blaney and Haughey, republican sympathies were going to play a major role. Into this situation came the first outbreak of violence in Northern Ireland.

Lynch was not well served by some of his cabinet at the time. His Minister for Justice, Micheál Ó Moráin, did not have any respect for him or for his office. Ó Moráin had a drink problem and was often absent from his office for long periods. The Secretary of the Department, Peter Berry, who was a most meticulous and dedicated public servant, was under the mistaken impression that his minister was passing on to Jack Lynch all the information that was coming into the department from the Garda Special Branch about the activities of certain of his ministers.

During all this period, Ó Moráin was drinking very heavily. He knew something very disturbing was happening among some of the colleagues in government. The one thing he could not believe was that Haughey was involved. One of the criticisms of him by Jack Lynch when he sacked him was that he did not inform him of the information he had been given by the Special Branch. Lynch told me that when he asked Ó Moráin why he didn't tell him, his reply was that he could not believe ministers were involved. Above all, he could not believe that Charlie Haughey was involved.

Captain Jimmy Kelly was an intelligence officer in the Irish Army who was linked with John Kelly OC of the Belfast Brigade of the Provisional IRA. Jimmy Kelly visited Belfast in August 1969. While there, he decided to travel to Derry and see what was going on. There was an Apprentice Boys march in Derry on 12 August. What he witnessed led him to throw in his lot with Northern nationalists. The predominant consideration for him was that nationalists had to be protected and the only way they could be protected was by providing them with guns. John Kelly, who was to play a major role in the operation, was part of a delegation that came to Dublin seeking guns.

People looking back on the situation forty years later, and with the trail of destruction in Northern Ireland in the meantime, might say that 'surely to God nobody was taking them seriously when they were asking for guns.' However, it was very hard at that time to refuse them guns because they were in a desperate situation. They were coming to Dublin almost daily. These delegations included people who would deny today any suggestion that they had ever sought guns. Delegations included successful Catholic businessmen and politicians such as Paddy Devlin who spoke from a platform in O'Connell Street while on their way to a meeting in Government Buildings. Devlin spoke of the need for guns in Northern Ireland. In his book, *Straight Left*, he said that he only once spoke publicly about the need for guns and he greatly regretted the speech. This delegation also included Paddy Kennedy, a Northern Ireland MP, whose name subsequently appeared on a bank account opened by the Department of Finance in Baggot Street, Dublin.

John Kelly, who was co-ordinator of the Defence Committee, also addressed the rally in O'Connell Street that day. He told later of meeting Jack Lynch, Paddy Hillery, Brian Lenihan and Neil Blaney, but not Charles Haughey at that time. Northern people, he said, were trying to find out if arms would be available in a worsening situation. John Kelly said that 'that was clearly understood from the beginning. We were getting an encouraging response that the Irish Government were sufficiently concerned to provide help if the situation worsened.' Again, in support of that contention, Eamonn McCann tells of a visit to his house in Derry by an officer who said that he represented the Irish army, and told McCann that the army was prepared to take men across the border into Donegal for training in the use of weapons. The men were brought across for training under cover of their being members of the FCA who might lead the people of the Bogside to defend themselves if they were supplied with arms. They were trained at Dunree Camp in Donegal. That programme was terminated very abruptly after about two weeks, when the newspapers heard about it.

Also included in these delegations was a shadowy figure called Jim Sullivan who was the chairman of the Central Citizens' Defence Committee in Belfast. He was a Marxist and a member of Official IRA. He later sat on Belfast City Council where he did extremely good work for the citizens of Belfast.

Many of these people from Northern Ireland were unknown to the Special Branch. For example, John Kelly became known to the Special Branch only when a customs officer spotted him on television at a meeting in the Gresham Hotel, protesting at the arrest of Haughey and Blaney. He remembered him as the man at Dublin Airport seeking the delivery of guns. He phoned the Special Branch who arrested him and detained him in the Bridewell for two days. Kelly states that he was not questioned for the duration of his arrest.

Another central character was Jim Gibbons, Minister for Defence. Prior to his appointment as Minister for Defence, Gibbons had been a junior minister in the Office of Public Works (under the Department of Finance). He had also been Colley's election agent in the leadership campaign against Haughey in 1966. When he was appointed junior minister in 1968, as a subordinate to Haughey in Finance, Haughey set out immediately to win him over. Haughey could be a very charming man when he wanted to be, both with men and women – particularly women.

When Gibbons became Minister for Defence, he still regarded himself as inferior to people like Haughey and Blaney. He had less experience than either even though he was of a similar age.

Blaney did not have any need to establish himself as a republican. His father had fought in the War for Independence and the Blaney name was well known in Donegal as representing a very strong republican voice. His regular journeys across the border brought him into daily contact with the effects of partition. He was greatly aggravated at being stopped by B-Specials and police patrols at border checkpoints, and he had a seething indignation at the situation in the six counties, and never recognised that the Northern Ireland state had any legitimacy.

There is a marvellous description of Neil Blaney in Tom McIntyre's book, *Through the Bridewell Gate*, which is the finest account of the Arms Trial. He is described as having 'a face like a Lurgan spade from which the humour will gradually drain through the years.' Never has a description been more accurate.

As the years passed, Blaney became less and less good humoured. He had lost his membership of Fianna Fáil, he no longer had an outlet for his very considerable talents, and his massive organisational skills which won Fianna Fáil many a seat in the Dáil were no longer in demand. Once he had made up his mind on any line of action, there was no going back. So, when the situation in Northern Ireland blew up, he felt that now was the time to intervene.

His views were shared by a man fashioned very like him – Kevin Boland, a dour individual who occasionally ventured out from his home in Rathcoole in later years to appear on RTÉ programmes where he launched periodic attacks on those he felt had let down the Republic.

Haughey's credentials were less obvious. He had never manifested any republican tendencies and few in Fianna Fáil would have been aware that his father had been a very active member of the Northern IRA and an officer of the lately formed Free State Army in 1922, and had smuggled 400 guns across the border from Donegal on the instructions of Michael Collins.

When the situation in Northern Ireland blew up, all of these characters were going about their business with various degrees of competence. They were thrown into a situation with which none of them was familiar and with which none of them knew how to deal. The result was considerable confusion.

⌘ ⌘ ⌘

On 6 May 1970, the country awoke to the startling news that Jack Lynch, had, in the early hours of that morning, sacked two of his most senior ministers, Charles J. Haughey, the Minister for Finance, and Neil Blaney, the Minister for Agriculture.

The public was taken completely by surprise, as were the newspaper reporters, who were unable to provide any convincing explanation of the development. I was woken from my sleep at

2 a.m. by loud knocking at my front door. The culprit was Ciarán MacKeon, then a sub-editor on the staff of *The Irish Press* and later to become well known as the founder, with Mairéad Corrigan, of the Peace Movement in Northern Ireland. Having failed to arouse me by phone, he had been instructed by the editor to take a taxi out to my house and to make sure that I arrived back in the office to prepare a story on the dramatic announcement by Jack Lynch, whose short statement did nothing to explain the reason for his drastic action against Haughey and Blaney.

On the journey into the city from Templeogue, Ciarán and I considered the possible reasons, reaching the conclusion that the development was almost certainly connected with the situation in Northern Ireland. Blaney had very strong views about British rule there and had been rebuked shortly before by Jack Lynch for his speech about Fianna Fáil policy on the possibility of armed insurrection .

Haughey's sacking was a complete surprise, however, and I felt that a serious mistake had been made. Haughey's name had never been associated with the republican wing of Fianna Fáil and a story, published by the IRA some time earlier, and suggesting that he had met the Chief of Staff, Cathal Goulding, and that a sum of £50,000 for the purchase of arms had been mentioned, was regarded by political journalists as being entirely mischievous. It was inconceivable that a man who, as Minister for Justice less than ten years earlier, had acted strongly to put members of the IRA behind bars would now be engaged in discussions with them about guns.

Outside the *Irish Press* office, I met a Fianna Fáil backbencher who expressed no surprise about the news regarding Haughey, but could not understand why the name of the Minister for Defence, Jim Gibbons, was not included in Jack Lynch's statement.

This intervention only confused the situation still further for me. The result was a story in that morning's *Irish Press* which asked more questions than it answered. All the other political writers were in the same boat. We had gone through several months of reporting the news at Leinster House since the siege of the Bogside in August 1969, completely unaware of the subterranean developments taking place around us. Even Liam Cosgrave's intervention in the Dáil on 5 May, when he asked the Taoiseach, Jack Lynch, if the sacking of Micheál Ó Moráin as Minister for Justice was the 'tip of the iceberg', had not alerted us to the extraordinary nature of the story that was about to break. We assumed that the departure of the minister was connected with an outburst by him against his hosts at a dinner of the Canadian Bar Association in the Shelbourne Hotel shortly before.

It was long afterwards that evidence emerged that Ó Moráin's sacking resulted from Lynch's accusation that he had failed as Minister for Justice to inform him of Special Branch reports linking a number of people, including members of the government, with an attempt to bring in guns illegally.

I returned to my bed at six o'clock and was awakened again two hours later by a call from RTÉ to take part in an early-morning discussion on the drama. Again, the discussion was conducted mainly in the dark about the reasons for the Taoiseach's action. None of us had any good explanation, which was not, also, libellous, and nobody in government was prepared to provide any information.

By eleven o'clock that morning, however, I felt I had sufficient information to say publicly on an RTÉ current affairs programme that the sackings were connected with an attempt to bring in guns for Northern Ireland through Dublin Airport. This was the first indication the public had of the background to the affair and, while I was happy that my information justified my going public on the matter, I remained worried until Jack Lynch told the Dáil that night that garda reports had linked Haughey and Blaney with attempts to import arms illegally. While nothing was proven, no shadow of suspicion must attach to any member of the government in a situation of this kind, he said.

Over the following days and weeks, bits of the story were being fitted together, but it was only after the court hearing of charges against a number of people suspected of being involved in the plot and the subsequent enquiry by the Dáil Committee of Public Accounts that a fuller picture emerged.

⌘ ⌘ ⌘

The story began in August 1969 when a parade by Apprentice Boys in Derry ended up with the inhabitants of the Bogside defending themselves with petrol bombs and stones against a very hostile mob of loyalists led by B-Specials and members of the RUC. For a number of days, nationalists were trapped in their homes, fearing for their lives. The siege of the Bogside lasted two days and brought to international attention leaders of the besieged community, such as Bernadette Devlin and Eamon McCann. It ended with the arrival of British troops on 14 August but, by that time, the trouble had spread to Belfast, where, within a few days, seven civilians were killed, including a seven-year-old boy, shot in the back while sleeping in his home in the Divis Flats. He was hit by a stray bullet fired by a B-Special from an armoured car which was driving up and down the road, firing indiscriminately. Nationalist areas, such as Bombay Street, were burned out.

Unfortunately, the situation in Belfast was precipitated by a small group of IRA men firing shots at an RUC station off Leeson Street, in order to divert attention away from Derry. In all of nationalist Belfast at that time there were ten guns. The attack on the RUC station brought the RUC and the B-Specials onto the streets, along with loyalist mobs who proceeded over the following days to attack nationalist areas, burning many of them to the ground. The nationalists were in a desperate situation and were clamouring for help from Dublin. The only help afforded to them by the government in Dublin was the sending of the army to border areas to set up field hospitals so that refugees could be assisted.

Many people in Northern Ireland thought that the army was going to come across the border. The unionist politician, John Taylor, was convinced that an invasion was imminent. However, the Irish army was incapable of invading any place in the six counties. It took some army lorries two days to reach the border from Cork. They kept breaking down and spare parts had to be sent to repair them. About the only place they could have captured was Newry, which they might have held overnight. There was no way that they could have taken Belfast or even Derry.

In Dublin, the Irish government was meeting on a regular basis, with general concern being expressed by ministers that something must be done, but nobody quite sure what needed to be done. Jack Lynch went on television to express the government's deep concern at the worsening situation in Northern Ireland and indicating that the Government 'would not stand by'. Over the years, this has become distorted to a claim that the Government would not stand 'idly by'. This statement was welcomed by people in Derry. The people in Belfast knew it was meaningless – in fact, it was inflaming the hatred of the loyalists and B-Specials against the nationalists.

Captain Jimmy Kelly witnessed what was happening in Derry and Belfast and returned to Dublin to report on the situation to his superior officer, Colonel Michael Hefferon, head of intelligence, a most honourable man whose name was damaged by this affair. Undoubtedly, he gave a great deal of latitude to Captain Jimmy Kelly to assist the people in Northern Ireland, but he was much influenced by the fact that Kelly had ready access to members of the Government and appeared to be taking his instructions from them. He told the Dáil Committee of Public Accounts subsequently that from around October 1969,

Kelly was not acting under his orders. Kelly told him that he had been instructed to act on behalf of the Government by Haughey and Blaney. His orders, he said, came from Haughey, Gibbons and Blaney. Colonel Hefferon believed what Kelly told him.

The Government was meeting three times a week at this stage. Some cabinet members were taking a very hawkish line, with Boland and Blaney being the most hawkish. It was claimed afterwards that Charles Haughey joined them in urging that the army be sent across the border. Haughey told me that he never took such a line as a solution to the problem and would have regarded such a development as highly dangerous on every front – that they would have been unable to assist the people in Northern Ireland and would have brought the conflict into this part of the island.

A Northern Ireland committee, chaired by Haughey, was set up by the Government but, according to other ministers, it met only once. Haughey and Gibbons were also given specific authority to build up the army to meet an emergency situation. The question arose, of course, as to what constituted an emergency situation. Over the years since, it became clear that the Government was prepared in a 'doomsday' situation to hand out guns to people in the nationalist population to defend themselves.

Captain Kelly, in the course of his evidence at the Arms Trial, disclosed that Jim Gibbons had issued a directive to the Army in February 1970, instructing it to be prepared to cross into Northern Ireland to hand out guns for the defence of the nationalists if the Government so decided. No trace of the directive could be found but Kelly's claim was confirmed by Michael Hefferon who had made a note of the directive and was able to read it into the court records. Thirty years later, the release of the Army files for the period provided further details.

After 1969, government ministers refused to talk about the possibility of a doomsday situation or any plans by the

Government to deal with the event, so that it came as something of a surprise to find the whole thing confirmed in the Army papers, with one important proviso that any help was to be provided out of existing resources. This proviso undermined claims that the directive provided authority for the purchase of arms to meet a possible doomsday situation.

While various ministers ran in fright from questions on the matter over the years, Des O'Malley made an important disclosure in a television interview in a programme made by RTÉ to mark the twenty-fifth anniversary of the Arms Crisis. In the programme Captain Jim Kelly was asked by Mike Milotte what the plans were for dealing with the situation in Northern Ireland. He said that a directive had been issued to the Army on 6 February 1970 by Gibbons, stating that the Army should prepare for a situation where it would have to move into the six counties to provide people in the civilian population with arms to defend themselves. O'Malley was questioned on what Kelly had said. He replied that that scenario could happen only in the event of a doomsday situation. The fact that he admitted it could happen was sufficient to prove the point. In order to provide for a doomsday situation, the Government had set aside 500 older weapons, which were replaced by newer and more up-to-date rifles.

In early April 1970, Jim Gibbons was contacted by Neil Blaney who told him that Ballymurphy in Belfast was under attack. It appeared to Blaney that the doomsday scenario had arisen and he persuaded Gibbons to the same effect. Gibbons contacted the Army to release the weapons. They were taken from Cathal Brugha barracks towards the border. At this stage, Jack Lynch was on his way to Cork for the weekend. En route, he was stopped by gardaí who told him that there was an urgent message for him. He took the call to learn that the arms were on their way up north. He immediately contacted Gibbons, telling him to countermand the order. The order was countermanded and the guns were taken into Dundalk barracks and kept there for the duration.

Clearly, it was never the intention of the Government to go into Northern Ireland, except in a doomsday situation. The question, of course, was who was going to decide what was a doomsday situation. Only Blaney and Boland seemed to have favoured intervention when the first outbreak of violence occurred in August 1969.

⌘　　⌘　　⌘

In August 1969, I was sent to Belfast by the *Irish Press* to write a story on the aftermath of the attacks on nationalist areas by crowds of loyalists, supported by the B-Specials, in which seven people had been killed inside a week. Belfast was a frightened city. Tensions were extremely high, with Catholic areas expecting renewed attacks each night. The arrival of the British Army had brought some relief, but the general feeling among the nationalist population was that they would have to defend themselves.

I was standing on the footpath outside the *Irish Press* office when a car pulled up beside me. The driver introduced himself to me as a Catholic doctor who was extremely worried about the safety of his people in case of further attacks by loyalist mobs. He recognised me from my television appearances on RTÉ and he wished to express his concern at the effect the speech by Jack Lynch on RTÉ the previous week had had in Belfast. It might be very helpful to the people in Derry or in Newry to tell them that the Irish Government would not stand by in the face of attacks on Catholic areas, he said, but the people in Belfast knew that the Irish Government could not come to their aid. Statements of this kind, he went on, merely inflamed loyalist attitudes, while they did nothing to alleviate the anxieties of the Catholic population.

I spent a couple of days in Belfast, during which I met for the first time Captain James Kelly, who was introduced to me at the *Irish Press* office by a colleague, Seamus Brady, who had joined the staff of *The Irish Press* after having worked for a number of years for the *Daily Express*. Brady was friendly with Neil Blaney, and was also regarded as having good contacts with a number of other ministers.

On the evening before I left Belfast, I was having a drink at the bar in my hotel when I was approached by a man whom I had met on a previous visit to Belfast and who was employed by a semi-state company as its representative in Belfast. He asked me if I would meet the chairman of the Citizens' Defence Committee, Jim Sullivan, later that evening. I agreed to the meeting and, at the appointed time, they both arrived at my room in the hotel.

The Committee leader quickly got down to business. He wanted to meet a member of the Irish Government to make him aware of the perilous nature of the situation facing the Catholic population of Belfast. In short, they wanted guns to defend themselves. Later, I learned that similar requests for guns were made to almost every journalist from Dublin visiting Belfast at that time.

I advised him that it was most unlikely that any government minister would be able to provide that kind of assistance. He became quite angry and assured me that they would get guns from whatever source, even if it involved stealing them from the Irish Army or the Garda Síochána, because, he said, 'I am never again going to allow my people to be subjected to the kind of assault launched on them last week by loyalist mobs.'

As I again advised him of the unlikelihood of their getting guns from Dublin, he said, 'You don't seem to realise how serious the situation here in Belfast is.' He thumped the table and went on, 'I'll try to tell you how serious the situation is. I ordered a man to be burned to death last Thursday night. He was a sniper on a high building firing into a Catholic area. We had no way to defend ourselves against him; so, I told my men to burn down the building. He was burned to death in the fire. It was a drastic action but there was no alternative. So, I am telling you again that we will get guns to defend ourselves.'

I did not know then nor was I aware for a long time afterwards that the Government had taken a tentative decision to provide weapons in an emergency or 'doomsday' situation. The first intimation of this development came in late September or early October with the news that citizens from Northern Ireland had been inducted into the FCA to be trained in the use of firearms at Fort Dunree in Donegal.

In my hotel room in Belfast, however, I was unaware of all this and could only tell my visitors that while I believed they would not be given guns, I would contact a member of Government to see if he would meet them. I suggested the name of George Colley, to which they were quite agreeable, but then I remembered that he was due to go to a meeting of the World Bank that week and I put forward the name of Neil Blaney, to which they also agreed.

I met Blaney next day to acquaint him of the request for a meeting and also to inform him of the frightened state of the Catholic people in Belfast. He had reservations about meeting the Citizens' Defence leader whom he regarded as a member of the Marxist wing of the IRA. He told me that there was already in existence the nucleus of a nationalist Catholic-oriented group. I got the impression that he would prefer to do business with this group, but, nonetheless, he agreed to meet the Belfast people. Before I left him, he suggested that I might go and tell Jack Lynch about the situation in Belfast, but I told him that I had been asked to convey a request for a meeting and, having fulfilled that task, I did not wish to take the matter any further.

About a week later, my colleague, Arthur Noonan, told me that he had seen two of my Belfast contacts, whom he recognised from newspaper photographs, standing outside Government Buildings. I knew then that the meeting with Neil Blaney had taken place.

There were sporadic outbursts of violence in Northern

Ireland in the succeeding months but I never knew and never enquired what response had been given to my Belfast contacts. Some government ministers have told me that all the delegations were informed that guns would not be made available, but many of the Northern representatives believed that the Government would not let them down in an emergency situation.

I asked Blaney on one occasion about the situation at the time. He told me that the situation was now under control. I expressed my anxiety at the conflict that could develop if too many guns were on the loose in Northern Ireland. He told me that there was nothing to worry about; everything was under control.

In October 1969, an article in the Official IRA newspaper claimed that the Chief of Staff, Cathal Goulding had had a meeting with the Minister for Finance, Charles Haughey, at which it had been suggested by Haughey that a sum of £50,000 was available for the purchase of guns for the defence of nationalists in Northern Ireland. Accompanying the article were a number of photographs of government ministers, claiming that all of them knew about Haughey's offer and asking the pertinent question, 'How can Lynch not know?' The editor of *The Irish Press*, Tim Pat Coogan, drew the matter to my attention, asking me if I thought there was any truth in the story. My immediate reaction was to reject it out of hand and to suggest that it was a mischievous attempt to damage Haughey. Coogan agreed. The possibility of Haughey being involved in this kind of operation with Cathal Goulding was too far-fetched to be credible.

About this time, Ó Moráin, following a conversation with Berry, raised a question in cabinet about a member of the Government meeting with known IRA leaders. Haughey immediately owned up to a casual meeting with Cathal Goulding, but claimed that there was nothing to it. Ó Moráin felt embarrassed for having raised the matter at all and no further questions were asked about it. None of the newspapers followed up the story.

Over twenty years later, the Citizens' Defence leader who had approached me in Belfast for guns and who, at that time, was close to Goulding in the Official IRA, claimed that he was present at the meeting in Dublin when Haughey made the offer to Goulding.

Events in Northern Ireland continued to impinge on politics in the Republic, with recurring rumours about guns being sent across the border, but no hard evidence emerged to substantiate these stories. The first real indication that all was not well in the Government came with the sacking of the Minister for Justice, Micheál Ó Moráin.

⌘ ⌘ ⌘

On 16 August 1969, Charles Haughey was given authority as Minister for Finance to provide financial assistance for the 'relief of the distress' in Northern Ireland. A sum of £100,000 was agreed by the Government and was voted retrospectively by the Dáil – the vote was actually taken in March 1970. Haughey was dispensing money out of the fund at the request of Jimmy Kelly who became the liaison officer between the people of Belfast and the Department of Finance. He was dealing primarily with a civil servant in the department, Tony Fagan, who was a most honourable man. He was totally loyal to Charles Haughey, whom he served as Private Secretary for a number of years.

Haughey never spoke to Fagan again after the Arms Trial. As far as Haughey was concerned, Tony Fagan became a non-person. Fagan suffered greatly from the fallout and later had a heart attack and retired prematurely from the civil service. He did not receive much sympathy from many of his colleagues in the civil service who regarded him as a man who had flown too close to the sun and got his wings burnt. He had crossed the line that should separate politician and civil servant.

An account was first opened in the Bank of Ireland in Clones where it was intended that money would be transferred to the Red Cross for relieving distress. The account was subsequently transferred to the Munster and Leinster Bank (later called AIB) in Baggot Street, Dublin, when it became clear that the Irish Red Cross had no authority to operate outside the state. The account was in the names of a number of people from Northern Ireland, including Paddy Devlin and Paddy Kennedy, who were MPs. John Kelly, OC Belfast Brigade, used some of the money to buy arms and to pay allowances to members of the IRA who were manning the barricades in Belfast and were unable to collect their dole. Some received small amounts of money, but most received nothing. There was a dispute as to how much was provided for arms. It is generally agreed that £60,000 was spent on arms purchased from a German dealer.

Money was paid into the Baggot Street account at the request of the defence committees and was all sanctioned by Charles J. Haughey. He subsequently claimed in the courts that he never knew that it was intended to buy guns. He said that it would be absolutely wrong if it was used for this purpose.

An important event was the holding of a meeting, on 4 October 1969, in Bailieboro, County Cavan, of representatives of defence committees. Captain Kelly was allegedly told by Haughey at a meeting in Kinsealy that a sum of £50,000 was available to buy guns. According to the Special Branch, Kelly used £500, given to him by Haughey, to buy food and drink for the Northern representatives.

The Special Branch told Peter Berry, Secretary of the Department of Justice, of the meeting in Bailieboro. At the time, Berry was in Mount Carmel Hospital, where he had had an emergency operation. He tried to contact his minister, Micheál Ó Moráin, and the Taoiseach, Jack Lynch. Having failed to contact both men, he contacted Haughey, who pretended to know nothing about it but asked questions about the source of Berry's information.

John Kelly claimed that Jimmy Kelly, in meeting these people at Bailieboro, was acting on behalf of the Irish Government. The Official IRA was not acceptable to the Irish Government. The reason for the Bailieboro meeting was to set up a northern command which would be acceptable to the Irish Government and would be involved only in conflict in Northern Ireland, he said.

This was the basis on which Neil Blaney had been making speeches some months previously. It was legitimate, he said, for people within the six counties to take up arms to pursue the objective of a united Ireland.

The organisers of the Bailieboro meeting claimed that the intention was to set up a group within Northern Ireland that would not be Marxist or Official IRA, but would be the nucleus of a new organisation that was Catholic-oriented and would lead the nationalists in Northern Ireland in whatever way the Government here provided assistance.

On 16 October, 1969, the Garda Síochána further briefed Berry on the Bailieboro meeting. Berry, still at Mount Carmel Hospital, sent for Jack Lynch to inform him of the happenings in Bailieboro. Lynch later denied that any such conversation took place but was contradicted by Gibbons' evidence that, following a request to him for more information, he had gone to Hefferon. Gibbons did not come back to Lynch with the requested information and, like Lynch, seems to have forgotten completely about the whole matter.

The IRA in Northern Ireland divided shortly after the Bailieboro meeting. The divisions in the IRA first of all occurred in Belfast. The Official IRA was breaking up. It was headed by Billy McMillan. One of his subordinates, Billy McKee, later became the head of the Provisional IRA. Billy McMillan was a very likeable person, who was opposed to the violence of the Provisional IRA and particularly to its bombing campaign. To people like Blaney, Billy McMillan was totally unacceptable as a

Marxist. For similar reasons, Jim Sullivan was equally unacceptable.

Jim Sullivan appeared on a Northern Ireland television programme some years later where he claimed he had visited Haughey in Kinsealy. At this meeting, Haughey told him that £50,000 was available for the purchase of arms. Haughey disliked Jim Sullivan, which is not surprising as Sullivan was a rather aggressive individual who would have had no time for the niceties of Kinsealy. Haughey did not want to have any more dealings with him. Sullivan went back to Belfast and talked openly about money being available from the Irish Government to buy arms.

This information was passed on to British Intelligence who conveyed the information back to London. Haughey's name consequently became known to British intelligence possibly before it became known to the Special Branch in Dublin.

Des O'Malley stated on RTÉ that the mohair section of Fianna Fáil was more at home with the Provisionals than with the Marxist Official IRA. Seán Mac Stiofáin, who was Chief of Staff of the IRA, said that the split in the organisation was inevitable because the IRA refused to defend the people of Northern Ireland.

Efforts to buy guns in London and New York in late 1969 were not successful and attention switched to Hamburg and arms dealer Otto Schleuter, described by John Kelly as 'a most unsavoury character'. Albert Luykx, owner of the Sutton Park Hotel and a friend of Blaney's, became involved. Luykx agreed to act as a liaison officer with arms dealers in Germany because he knew the people and the language. He made contact with Schleuter about whom John Kelly was very suspicious, having paid money to him and not received any arms. On a few occasions, guns were supposed to come in and small boats were sent out to Kish lighthouse to meet passing trawlers to take in weapons. However, no guns ever came.

On 25 March 1970, a big consignment of arms was supposed to be landed at Dublin Port from Antwerp by way of a vessel called the *City of Dublin*. This is one of the most important developments in the whole story. It had been decided at this stage to go about the business in an official way and Haughey was asked, as Minister for Finance, to arrange for clearance of the cargo. Haughey told Tony Fagan to arrange with customs for the admission of a cargo of mild steel plate, without customs examination. Haughey claimed subsequently that he knew nothing of the contents of this cargo.

Captain Jimmy Kelly was at Dublin Port with a truck supplied by a politician. The guns were to be brought to a rendezvous on this side of the border where, according to Captain Kelly, they were to be kept under his control until such time as the Government decided that a doomsday situation had arrived. There was also a group of recruits from the Provisional IRA standing by at Dublin Port with a truck. This group intended to seize the weapons and take them straight across the border into the six counties.

Again, the guns never arrived, this time because an end user's certificate was not at the point of embarkation. John Kelly says of this failed attempt: 'We had men in trucks waiting to pick them up under the supervision of Jim Kelly. They were to be taken to a designated location near the border for distribution if a doomsday situation developed. There were other plans by republicans to take the guns directly into the North.'

Seán Mac Stiofáin told RTÉ: 'There was a unit of IRA volunteers from Northern Ireland standing by to take the guns and put them into IRA camps. Certainly, the IRA was going to take the guns for itself.'

Jimmy Kelly and John Kelly asked to see the ship's manifest where it showed that the items were listed for loading in Antwerp but the guns and ammunition had been crossed out. All that was left of the consignment was a carton of flak jackets, which Jimmy

Kelly took possession of and brought to his house in Dublin where he stored them. Subsequently, Mac Stiofáin arrived at his house, asked for the flak jackets, put them in the boot of his car and drove away with them. This action casts doubt on the claim that everything that was brought in was to be kept under the control of the army.

The extraordinary thing is that the army itself collected a consignment of guns that very same day. While Captain Jimmy Kelly and his men were waiting on the docks for their consignment from Antwerp, a lowly sergeant was also waiting with eight privates for a consignment on behalf of the Irish Army. His consignment duly arrived and he drove away with the weapons because all the documentation was in order. However, for Captain Kelly and his men, nothing was in order.

Prior to this, on 6 February 1970, Jim Gibbons had issued a new directive to the Irish Army, and Jimmy Kelly relied on this to a large extent to claim that he had government authority to bring in arms. The new directive, which was recorded by the Chief of Staff of the army and by the Head of Intelligence, Michael Hefferon, was to the effect that the army must prepare itself for a contingency situation in which it would not only have to move across the border to help the nationalist population, but would also provide weapons for the nationalists to defend themselves.

Before Jim Kelly went to Hamburg to contact Schleuter, together with Luykx and John Kelly, his commanding officer, Michael Hefferon, rang the Minister for Defence, Jim Gibbons, to tell him that Kelly was about to embark on a mission to the continent to vet weapons. Gibbons at this stage knew that Captain Kelly was throwing his lot in with the Northern nationalists, and he decided that the best thing to do was to get Kelly out of the army. However, he knew that Kelly had a wife and family and he says that he didn't want him to lose his job and be left with no means of living. He went to Haughey to ask him whether there was any job that could be given to Kelly. Haughey said that he had the ideal job for him: a pig-smuggling preventive officer at the border. Gibbons was happy with this and never made any further enquiries. The post never materialised and Kelly continued in the Army, working on behalf of the Northern defence committees to secure arms, with the claim that he was operating with the full authority of the Irish Government.

In early April 1970, fighting had broken out in Ballymurphy in Belfast, with fears of a doomsday situation. Gibbons ordered the 500 army rifles which had been set aside by the Government to be transported to the border. Subsequently in court he refused to say why the guns were going to the border. Despite the efforts of counsel over a number of days to get him to admit that they were going across the border, he refused to admit that. His refusal is understandable as it would have left the Government open to the charge of intervention in the affairs of another state, contrary to international agreement. Consequently he evaded the question, and counsel for the defence eventually gave up.

With the attempt having failed to bring guns into Dublin Port, the focus now switched to Vienna and an attempt to bring the guns in by air. In early April 1970, Jim Kelly went to Vienna to inspect guns that were on offer, again from the arms dealer, Schleuter. He eventually managed to obtain a number of revolvers for which Schleuter claimed he had the licences in Vienna. Schleuter said that he had heavier weapons for sale but that he would issue them only from Spain where he had the licences. Jimmy Kelly bought a consignment of small arms.

John Kelly went to Dublin Airport to collect the guns when they arrived from Vienna. He was to tell customs that he was acting on behalf of the Department of Finance and that this was an official importation. But bringing the guns in by air proved no easier than the attempts to bring them in by sea. Efforts to engage a charter plane failed and those involved seemed to be unaware until the last moment that passenger planes were not permitted to transport guns and ammunition. When an official at Dublin Airport learned that it was intended to use an Aer Lingus passenger plane to transport the guns, he rang a number of government departments to ascertain if permission had been obtained to override IATA rules on the matter. The only two departments which had permission to bring in guns, Justice and Defence, knew nothing about any consignment. The Special Branch was informed and 'a ring of steel' was thrown around the airport, which led Micheál Ó Moráin to ask the question, 'Where the hell do they think we are – fucking Casablanca?'

Peter Berry later told the Arms Trial that, on hearing of this development, Haughey rang, and asked him if the consignment could be allowed in if it went straight to Northern Ireland, to which Berry said 'no' – it would be seized as soon as it landed. Haughey denied that any such conversation took place.

Jim Kelly, who was waiting in Vienna for instructions, says he got orders from Haughey to call off the entire operation. Haughey denied Kelly's account, thereby putting Kelly's defence that he was acting under government instructions at all times, at considerable risk.

In May 1970, the leader of the opposition, Liam Cosgrave, got a note on Garda-headed notepaper, naming Haughey, Blaney, Jim Kelly, Michael Hefferon and Jim Gibbons as being involved in a plot to smuggle guns into the state. Having failed to get the *Irish Independent* and the *Sunday Independent* interested, Cosgrave confronted Lynch with his information. Lynch denied the involvement of Gibbons and Hefferon but, during the early hours of 6 May, he announced that Blaney and Haughey had been sacked on suspicion of involvement.

After his acquittal and in the euphoric atmosphere of the occasion as he was carried from the courtroom, Haughey called on those who had brought the court proceedings to do the honourable thing, which was generally taken to mean that Jack Lynch should resign. Lynch, who was in New York at the time attending a meeting at the United Nations, immediately replied: 'If that is a challenge, I will meet it head-on.' Haughey had made a serious miscalculation, as he discovered from the newspapers the following Sunday morning when all of the lead stories indicated that Lynch intended to take up Haughey's challenge.

On Monday morning, Lynch arrived home from New York to be met by a huge crowd of Fianna Fáil deputies, senators and general supporters. Any hope that Haughey had of undermining Lynch's position was dashed and he was to remain banished from the central core of Fianna Fáil in the Dáil for the next five years. But he used the time fruitfully, first by getting himself elected at the Árd Fheis of the party to the comparatively lowly and, for him, humiliating position of vice-president, of which title there were a number of holders. However, this position enabled him to travel the country, cultivating the friendship and support of branches in every constituency, with the result that when Fianna Fáil returned to power in1977, many of the new breed of Dáil deputies were people whom Haughey had cultivated on the rubber chicken circuit in the previous years.

The rural support also led to a growing campaign in 1974–75 for the restoration of Haughey to a very unimpressive Fianna Fáil front bench in the Dáil. Lynch allowed himself to be influenced by the calls for Haughey's return and, in the naive belief that Haughey had changed and was now willing to be part of the team, he appointed him as spokesman on Health.

Haughey never spoke again about his role in the Arms Crisis and refused to be interviewed about it. On at least one occasion, he threatened the interviewer on an RTÉ television programme that if he raised any question about the subject, he would immediately get up from his seat and walk off the set.

Information did emerge over the years, however, to clarify the situation. Kevin Boland, in an interview with Vincent Browne, related how Haughey had approached him early in 1970 before the whole story broke, to tell him of the plans to bring in guns from abroad. Boland claimed to have advised Haughey that that would be a most unwise activity and that if it were to be done, it should be only with the full approval of the Government.

The two Kellys, John and Jim, also told Vincent Browne of being shocked by Haughey's evidence at the trial. Both men said that they felt they had been betrayed. Haughey's evidence was especially damaging for Jim Kelly, who said that he had rung Haughey from Vienna for instructions as to his next move after he had failed to get the guns on an Aer Lingus flight to Dublin. Haughey denied the phone call, which was later confirmed by his private secretary, Tony Fagan, at the Public Accounts Committee hearing. By his denial, he was seriously undermining Kelly's defence that he was acting at all times on the orders of the Government.

⌘　　⌘　　⌘

The Arms Crisis pushed Jim Gibbons reluctantly into the spotlight, which remained on him during the rest of his life and will continue to focus on him in historical analysis as students try to unravel the mysteries of the most intriguing political drama of our time.

His prominence in the story arises from his period as Minister for Defence in the crucial year 1969–70. The Northern problem, ignored by successive Irish governments for years, with the exception of rhetorical speeches by party leaders on the occasion of anniversary functions, suddenly blew up in the faces of Irish politicians, with the siege of the Bogside.

The Government met in emergency session and continued to meet on an almost daily basis as the ministers tried to grapple with an unfamiliar and very confusing situation. The instruction to the army to set aside 500 older rifles, together with the initial recruitment and training of young Derry men by the Donegal FCA, confirms that the Government was ready to take drastic action if a 'doomsday situation' arose.

In the meantime, delegations of all kinds were arriving daily in Dublin, seeking the assistance of the Government. They were quite explicit in the type of assistance they required – it was always guns. Food and clothing were secondary to the overwhelming demand for guns. All of these people seem to have gone home to Belfast in the belief that the Government 'would not let them down'.

Captain James Kelly, had also arrived on the scene at this time and it was his involvement that brought Jim Gibbons, as Minister for Defence, directly into the picture. In August 1969, the young Army intelligence officer reported to his immediate Army superior, Colonel Michael Hefferon, graphic details of the situation in Derry and Belfast. Colonel Hefferon, in turn, reported the situation to his minister, Jim Gibbons, who for the first time became aware of the existence of Captain Kelly. Before long, he was to get to know him personally, as he became a regular visitor to Government Buildings to meet the Minister for Agriculture, Neil Blaney, and to liaise with the Minister for Finance, Charles Haughey, in regard to requests for financial aid from the £100,000 Government fund. Leaders of the defence committees in Northern Ireland claimed afterwards that it was generally accepted that the money was being sought for the purchase of guns; Haughey, however, claimed that he had no knowledge that the money was issued for any purpose other than the relief of distress, such as the purchase of clothes and food.

The Special Branch was gradually building up a file through informants and by surveillance of the main characters in the operation. Captain Kelly's name began appearing in reports and when he chaired the meeting of leaders of Northern Defence Committees in Bailieboro, County Cavan, a detailed report of the meeting was sent to the Secretary of the Department of Justice, Peter Berry. The report alleged that the Northern representatives were members of subversive organisations – which was correct in so far as many of the defence committee leaders were also members of the IRA. It was also alleged that statements had been made at the meeting that substantial amounts of money were available for the purchase of guns.

Jack Lynch later denied any memory of meeting Peter Berry at Mount Carmel Hospital, and being informed about the report, but there is evidence to suggest that he asked Jim Gibbons to investigate the report and that Gibbons contacted Colonel Hefferon about the matter. Neither Gibbons nor Hefferon, apparently, ever came back to Lynch with a report. With so many other matters on his mind about the Northern troubles, it is not surprising that the Taoiseach forgot about a story involving a comparatively junior army officer, which, he felt, should have been dealt with by the officer's immediate superiors. As he said later, 'If the law is being broken, let the gardaí do their job.'

On 25 March, Captain Kelly told Gibbons of the failed attempt to bring in guns on a ship through Dublin Port. Gibbons did not, apparently, know at that time about the properly authorised consignment of guns for the army which had arrived at the docks that same day for delivery to army barracks in Dublin. Kelly knew of it though, as he had spoken on the quays to the platoon involved in collecting the consignment. It is surprising that more prominence was not given to this aspect of the story in the arms trial.

Neither could Gibbons have known, and it is not clear that Captain Kelly was aware, of the presence and intentions of Northern Ireland IRA members also waiting at the docks.

Gibbons next came into the story a month later when he learned of the attempt to bring in guns through Dublin Airport. He claimed that he immediately went to Haughey and asked him to call the whole thing off, to which Haughey replied that he would call it off for a month. Gibbons then claimed that he said, 'For God's sake, call it off altogether.'

Haughey denied at the subsequent Arms Trial that this

conversation ever took place and the trial judge, Seamus Henchy, told the jury that the different accounts by the two men could not be reconciled by any suggestion of a lapse of memory. One of the two must be lying. It was surprising that the presiding judge referred only to the conflict of evidence between Haughey and Gibbons when, in fact, Haughey's evidence also conflicted with the evidence of Peter Berry, Tony Fagan and his co-defendant, Captain Jim Kelly. For Haughey to be telling the truth, the other four all had to be telling lies.

When Haughey was acquitted by the jury, Gibbons suffered greatly from the belief that the public regarded him as a perjurer. This suffering was eased only when Haughey was exposed as a liar at the McCracken Tribunal in 2001.

Gibbons had to suffer, also, from the knowledge that he had not been a very convincing witness at the trial in two particular respects. He was put in the almost impossible position as a prosecution witness of having to explain his actions in regard to a new directive to the army in February 1970 and to instructions, on 2 April 1970, to send up to the border the 500 weapons, which had been put into cold storage by the Government in August 1969. These were both extremely ambivalent actions, involving, as they did, possible interference in the affairs of another state, which carried the gravest implications in international law. Gibbons was forced, in the circumstances, to evade a succession of leading questions from defence lawyers, in order to avoid an admission that the Government had contemplated actions with the most disturbing consequences.

He could not admit that, on 6 February 1970, he had issued a new directive to the army to be prepared not only for possible intervention in Northern Ireland, but for the handing over of weapons to Northern citizens to defend themselves against murderous attacks. Neither could he admit the purpose of sending 500 guns to the border in April 1970. This latter action was inspired by an alarming call from Neil Blaney to Gibbons that Ballymurphy was being attacked and that the 'doomsday' they had feared had arrived. The order to dispatch the guns from Dublin was countermanded only when Jack Lynch intervened.

Before the Arms Crisis, Jim Gibbons was a comparatively cheerful and friendly personality who, along with Sean Dunne and Pat Lindsay, gave endless enjoyment to the political correspondents at Leinster House, when he would join their table in the restaurant for afternoon tea and the three wonderful raconteurs would compete with one another to tell the best story. His detailed accounts of the behaviour of some of his colleagues at meetings of the Council of Europe in Strasbourg were hilarious.

After the event, he became taciturn and introspective. He refused to speak to me for three years because I had suggested when the story broke in 1969 that he had questions to answer. It was only at a meeting in Strasbourg about 1973 that our relationship was restored.

It appeared to those who knew him that he was in a dilemma at the time of the Arms Crisis. It was not a time when a member of the Government could give an impression of being less patriotic than his colleagues. Gibbons was a member of a Kilkenny family with a long tradition of Republicanism. He was inclined to express himself at times with considerable vehemence. John Kelly met him only once or twice but he said on one occasion that 'Gibbon's vehemence frightened me.' A colleague in government remembers him as thumping the table to make his point. He was aware of the actions of Captain Jimmy Kelly in trying to assist Northern nationalists to obtain guns but appears to have made no effort to stop him.

The Taoiseach, Jack Lynch, could not understand why Giboons did not disclose to him the activities of Blaney and Haughey but it appears that he was relying on the older and more experienced man from Mayo, Micheál Ó Moráin, who, as Minister for Justice, had more detailed information, to inform

Lynch. He told of going to Ó Moráin on one occasion to ask him if he had told the Taoiseach, to which the Minister for Justice replied, 'No, not yet.'

The defence of the two Kellys, Jimmy and John, and Albert Luykx at the Arms Trial was that their actions had at all times had government authority and that they were acting in accordance with government policy. Their counsel claimed that the Minister for Defence, Jim Gibbons, did not have to sign any document to authorise their actions; all that was necessary was a nod of the head. Since Gibbons did not say 'no', counsel argued, it could be inferred that he was saying 'yes'. If this were the case, the question immediately arose as to why guns purchased with money from the Department of Finance failed to be loaded on board a ship in Antwerp in March 1975, and why they also failed to be loaded on board a plane at Vienna a month later. All the nodding in the world could not make up for the absence of the necessary documentation.

In any case, no Dublin jury was ever going to find the defendants guilty of wrongdoing in the circumstances that prevailed in Northern Ireland in the period 1969–70.

⌘　　⌘　　⌘

Jack Lynch was frequently upset at the line followed by commentators on the Arms Crisis, particularly on television programmes. A constant theme was that Lynch knew about the conspiracy all along but gave Blaney and Haughey sufficient rope to hang themselves.

He was especially angry with a *Spotlight* programme by BBC Northern Ireland which repeated these allegations, supported by a number of academics who claimed that there was growing evidence to support the suggestions. He approached me to discuss the situation and to talk about the best way of combating these types of accusation. I suggested to him that he was partly to blame for the problem since he had not put on record his own account of events and, consequently, commentators felt entitled to speculate on events. I suggested to him that he was constantly trying to catch up with commentaries which he could have anticipated had his own account of events been on the record. I advised him even at that late stage to put down on paper his own memoirs or, if he preferred it, to dictate his memoirs onto a tape with the assistance of some trusted friends who could help to revive his memory of the times. I suggested a number of names to him and he agreed to think about it, but, unfortunately, he fell ill before he could do anything about it.

The central theme in the *Spotlight* programme was that Lynch was fully aware of the involvement of members of his government in the attempt to import arms illegally into the state and that the attempt was, in fact, a government-authorised operation. However, nobody on the programme asked the question as to why a government which regularly imported guns for the use of the state's security forces should resort to a most bizarre and impractical exercise to bring in guns from a very dubious dealer in Hamburg when it could so easily have obtained all the weapons it wanted through the normal channels.

Information was refused against Blaney in the District Court and he was discharged. All the others, except Haughey, defended their actions on the grounds that they were acting in accordance with government policy and with full authority. Haughey alone claimed that he knew nothing about the operation and was quite unaware that his co-defendants were engaged in trying to bring in guns into Dublin. All four were found not guilty by a jury.

Given the 'doomsday' commitment, it was hardly surprising that the two Kellys regarded their activities as being in accordance with government policy. In an interview in *The Irish Times* some years ago, John Kelly repeated his conviction that Jack Lynch knew all about the operation and that his actions and those of his co-accused were authorised by the Government. The logic of this interpretation is that other members of the Government, such as Paddy Hillery, Erskine Childers, George Colley and Padraig Faulkner, were also party to the exercise and approved of it. Having known all of these people and being aware of the strength of their hostility to a body like the Provisional IRA, I find it impossible to believe that they would have approved of a clandestine operation of this kind, involving dealings with an arms merchant in Hamburg whom John Kelly has described as 'a most unsavoury character'.

Moreover, in view of the fact that he had regular access to Government Buildings,and to senior ministers, Neil Blaney and Charles Haughey, it was difficult for Captain Kelly to believe other than that he was acting with full government authority. He was also reporting to his superior officer, Colonel Michael Hefferon, on the understanding that his reports were being passed on to the Minister for Defence, Jim Gibbons, for submission to the cabinet. There is no evidence that Gibbons, who was rightly worried about what was happening, ever tried to stop Kelly's activities or to tell Colonel Hefferon to bring them to an end.

Neither is it surprising that the note which was eventually sent by the Garda Síochána to the Fine Gael leader, Liam Cosgrave, in May 1970, named Gibbons and Hefferon as being involved with the others in the conspiracy. The first thing that Lynch said to Cosgrave when the garda note was drawn to his attention was that Gibbons and Hefferon were not involved. Had they been involved, of course, a prosecution could not have been brought against the others because Gibbons and Hefferon would have been seen to have been acting, and to have had the authority to do so, on behalf of the Department of Defence. Their involvement would have legitimised the entire affair. It could be said that while neither of them played any role in the clandestine operation, they knew it was in progress and did not try to stop it. Hefferon believed, as he swore in evidence, that Kelly was acting on behalf of the Government and was taking his orders directly from senior members of the Government. Gibbons' failure to inform Lynch of what was happening was governed by a number of factors among them the belief that it was the responsibility of the Minister for Justice, Micheál Ó Moráin, to convey the information he was receiving from the Special Branch, to the Taoiseach and to the Government. We have Gibbons' evidence that he tried to fix Kelly up with a job outside the Army, that he went to Haughey and appealed to him to call off the whole operation and that he went to Ó Moráin and asked him if he had told Lynch.

The major question remains – how much did Lynch know and when did he know? One of the more disquieting things about the *Spotlight* programme, from a historical perspective, was the assertion by Professor Henry Patterson from the University of Ulster, that, 'we are increasingly getting evidence that Lynch broadly knew what was going on and that he was dealing out enough rope to Haughey and Blaney to hang themselves.' There may well be a growing perception but there is no positive evidence to support this viewpoint.

There are things he should have known, and he should have exercised more authority over individual members of the Government, but he exercised a hands-off approach to his ministers in the knowledge that many of them had more experience than he had, and he believed that they would act at all times in the interests of the state. Like most other people at the time, he could not believe the garda reports which Peter Berry eventually brought to his attention in April 1970. Berry himself had great difficulty in coming to terms with the fact that Haughey, whom he had admired greatly in his previous role as Minister for Justice, was being named regularly in the garda reports.

Lynch was greatly shocked at the reports and would have preferred to have kept the whole affair quiet while privately rebuking Haughey and Blaney, but the matter was taken out of his hands when Liam Cosgrave made him aware of the garda note and when, more significantly, the Garda Síochána, fearing the whole thing would be hushed up, arrested Captain Kelly.

Lynch told me shortly afterwards that he lost all trust in people after the event. I suggested to him that there were many people around whom he could trust, to which he replied, 'How can you expect me to trust anybody after what has happened?' He told me also of Ó Moráin's assertion, just before he was sacked as Minister for Justice, that he had not told Lynch of the reports because he could not believe that members of the Government, and especially, Haughey, would be involved in an operation of this kind.

⌘   ⌘   ⌘

The most surprising thing about the State Papers on the Arms Crisis is not so much what they reveal as that they were released at all, in view of the extent of the efforts over the past thirty years to prevent the disclosure of their contents.

Since 1970, members of the Government of that period refused to talk about these events. The word 'doomsday' was a dirty word. Politicians fled almost in panic at its mention, and efforts to get any material on the record, if only for archival purposes, were rebuffed. Journalists who talked and wrote about the events of l969–70 had no evidence to back up their claims. The only supporting evidence came from the Arms Trial and Jim Gibbons' admission under pressure, and having failed to secure an order from the judge on the question of privilege, that he had issued a directive to the army to prepare for incursions into Northern Ireland if the need arose. Later in the trial, it emerged that the directive had been lost. No trace of it could be found despite an intensive search of all the likely locations. The court had to rely on the memory of Colonel Michael Hefferon, Head of Intelligence, for the contents of the directive which he had checked with army headquarters. Journalists had to assume that Gibbons would not have issued the directive unless it had been decided as government policy.

All these assumptions were made in the absence of any concrete evidence and the refusal of any government member or spokesman to talk about the matter. It was generally believed that no note had been kept of the government decision, or that any such note had been destroyed to preserve its secrecy. It was also believed that the army had destroyed any copy of the directive in the interests of security.

All was revealed in a series of documents from the army archives, which manage to convey the impression that while the Government was less than certain about what was going on and how it should react, the army was approaching the problem from a very practical and down-to-earth angle. For instance, a week after Gibbons issued the directive of 6 February 1970, the Chief of Staff, Sean McKeown, was back to him to ask a number of very relevant questions, including a hugely important one in regard to the legislative powers under which the army would be operating, bearing in mind that the army had already concluded that any action in crossing the border would be contrary to international law and the UN Charter. Gibbons, apparently, indicated that special emergency legislation would be introduced.

It was the absence of such legislation that enabled the Chief of Staff to state categorically in the files that there was no intention, in April 1970, of handing over to civilians in Northern Ireland the weapons sent to Dundalk from Dublin on Gibbons' orders. Although the army papers make no reference to it, it is interesting to note that the common belief that Jack Lynch who was, like Gibbons, stopped by gardaí on his way home in April 1970, with Blaney's apocalyptic message about Ballymurphy, countermanded Gibbons' order and that, as a result, the guns were stopped at Dundalk.

Gibbons' explanation that he ordered the guns from Dublin

in order to get Blaney 'off his neck' sounds remarkably weak and can have done little to lift army morale after his earlier declaration to the Chief of Staff that he had no idea of the extent of the assistance that would be needed by the Northern minority in the event of an emergency. One would have assumed that all of the relevant agencies and officials from the different departments would have been assembled by that time to draw up estimates of the needs of the minority in Northern Ireland, even allowing for the widespread ignorance down here of the situation less that one hundred miles away.

Supporters of the two sides in the Arms Crisis will draw different kinds of comfort from the army documents, but there is nothing in them to support the claim that Haughey and Blaney had been given carte blanche by the Government to do as they pleased and to spend the £100,000 government relief fund on the purchase of weapons from a very dubious arms dealer in Hamburg, to be handed out to civilians in Northern Ireland.

Such a development would have been unthinkable to Jack Lynch, who was horrified when he eventually learned of the plan. Equally, Paddy Hillery, Erskine Childers, George Colley, Padraig Faulkner, Paddy Lalor and other members of that government would have been shocked. However, it is obvious that the level of control from the top was not firm and that more control should have been exercised. The least that would have been required was the provision of regular reports from the two committees set up – one to consider the immediate needs of the army, headed up by Haughey and Gibbons; and the other dealing specifically with the Northern situation, whose members included Blaney, Haughey, Joe Brennan and Padraig Faulkner, and which met only once.

The general impression at the time, which is confirmed to some extent by these state papers, is of a government in almost permanent confusion, which was lucky to have a matter-of-fact army at its disposal, led by a group of officers under the Chief of

Staff, Sean MacKeown, who were not easily going to allow the men under their command to be exposed to danger.

The release of cabinet papers may in time redress the balance, but the failure up to now of any member of that Government to go on the record is not encouraging. The general belief is that very little, if any, record of cabinet discussions is available and that much of the discussion may not have been noted. Just as I attempted to persuade Jack Lynch to write down his memories of the time, equally, I tried and failed to get other members of his Government to go on the record, if only for the historical archives.

The army archives are not, of course, deliberately manufactured to show the army in a better light than its political masters, but that is the picture that emerges.

The most recent disclosures in the army archives on the Arms Crisis are valuable additions to our store of information, but they also add to the danger of complicating an already very confused situation. Further information is likely to be disclosed on a regular basis in the future under the 30-year rule and under the Freedom of Information legislation, so that it will be necessary from time to time for students of history and politics to reappraise the material.

The most recent discussion among commentators has concentrated on what Jack Lynch knew and when he knew it. The disclosure of the Lynch memos in *The Irish Times* represented a repeat, almost word for word, of a statement he made in the Dáil at the time of the publication in *Magill* of the Berry Diaries in May 1980.

For those people who were convinced that Lynch knew from the start of the involvement of members of his Government in the plot to import arms, the memos did nothing to lessen their conviction.

For some people, however, who were always convinced of Lynch's honesty and of his complete surprise on learning from

Peter Berry, the Secretary of the Department of Justice, in April 1970, of the involvement of ministers in the conspiracy, it led to a renewed study of the evidence. The conviction of Lynch's critics arises mainly from Peter Berry's claim that he gave Lynch information in October 1969, which should have alerted him to the situation.

The only evidence we have of information conveyed by Berry to Lynch in most bizarre circumstances as a patient about to undergo a major operation in Mount Carmel Hospital on 17 October 1969, was that an army officer had attended a meeting in Bailieboro, County Cavan, attended by heads of Defence Committees from Northern Ireland and had promised them £50,000 to buy guns for their defence.

There is no evidence that members of the Government were mentioned by Berry, nor could they have been mentioned because it was two months later before the gardaí told the Minister for Justice, Micheál Ó Moráin, of their suspicions that Charlie Haughey was involved.

A report from the Committee of Public Accounts, just published, has revealed that Garda Commissioner Weymes and the head of the Special Branch, Chief Supt John Fleming, told the Minister for Justice, Ó Moráin, in mid-December 1969, of a meeting between Haughey and a senior IRA man. Ó Moráin told the gardaí to keep checking. In the case of the information conveyed by Berry to Lynch on the Bailieboro meeting, we know that Lynch contacted the Minister for Defence, Jim Gibbons, who contacted the army Head of Intelligence, Colonel Michael Hefferon, to make enquiries. There is no evidence that Gibbons ever responded to Lynch's request for information, nor is there any evidence so far of Hefferon responding to Gibbons' request.

The other argument now being advanced is that because Lynch knew about the directive given by Gibbons to the Chief of Staff, General Sean McKeown, on 6 February 1970 to prepare the army for incursions into Northern Ireland to hand out weapons to members of the Nationalist population in a doomsday situation, that he knew of the plan to import arms from the continent.

The argument is that the directive led to the importation of arms but there is nothing in the directive to support this argument. The question may be asked as to where were the weapons to come from that were to be handed out to Northern Nationalists if the situation warranted it? The answer would appear to be that the Government envisaged that the 500 older guns set aside by the army on Government orders in August, 1969 for such a situation should be sufficient to meet the occasion. The counter-argument is that these guns could be easily identified as former army weapons and that only non-identifiable guns should be used, but there is nothing in the wording of the directive to suggest that the Government had this in mind. Of course, had the Government at the time or since, admitted to their having reached a decision to intervene in a doomsday situation much confusion could have been avoided. It was only the recent release of the army papers of the period that confirmed the issuing of the army directive of 6 February 1970.

Captain Jim Kelly's evidence at the Arms Trial about the 6 February directive did not receive the attention it deserved. The directive, or a copy, could not be found and efforts were made by the prosecution to cast doubts on whether such a directive had ever existed. But, again, as in the case of Capt Kelly's evidence relating to Jim Gibbons' knowledge of events, the reliable and very impressive Michael Hefferon was on hand to corroborate. Jack Lynch is quite definite that the first he knew of the involvement of members of the Government in the arms plot was when Peter Berry came to him with the evidence on 20 April 1970. Peter Berry claims that he told him a week earlier on 13 April and that the Taoiseach appeared to be taken by surprise. Berry had been under the impression that his Minister, Micheál

Ó Moráin, had been informing the Taoiseach all along of the various pieces of information coming into the Department of Justice from the Garda Special Branch.

When the Special Branch told Peter Berry about the Bailieboro meeting, while he was awaiting his operation in Mount Carmel Hospital, Berry immediately tried to contact Jack Lynch, who was unavailable. In desperation he rang Charlie Haughey, who surprised Berry by asking him, not for details of the meeting, but for the source of his information. Later in 1969, Berry told Ó Moráin of a meeting which the Special Branch said took place between Haughey and Cathal Goulding, Chief of Staff of the IRA, at Haughey's residence in Kinsealy. The Branch obviously had Goulding under observation. Subsequently, Ó Moráin mentioned the meeting at a gathering of the Government. Haughey immediately dismissed the matter as a casual meeting of no consequence. Nobody else raised any question about it and Ó Moráin said later he felt embarrassed for raising the matter.

It became clear from the evidence at the Public Accounts Committee that the first intimation the Department of Justice had of Haughey's involvement in the plot was in mid-December 1969.

4 Political Profiles

The person in Fianna Fáil for whom I had the greatest liking and respect was George Colley. Not all my colleagues shared my enthusiasm but I found him over the years to be totally honest and utterly reliable. He shared with me a deep distrust of Haughey. This distrust was felt also by Garret FitzGerald, of Fine Gael, one of the brightest young men on the opposition benches, whose wife, Joan, exercised a great influence over his life and whose suspicions of Haughey's intentions were much greater than those of her husband.

On the Fine Gael side, I also became very friendly with the party leader, James Dillon. Shortly after his election to the leadership, I asked him for an interview. He refused on the grounds that he had never given an interview to an *Irish Press* journalist and did not intend to start now. I expressed regret at his decision but suggested that, as time passed and we got to know one another, we might become friends. In fact, we became quite close friends and, near the end of his career, he suggested to me that he had concluded that he and I were the only two people in Ireland who understood anything about politics.

He and I disagreed on the nature of the bitterness that persisted from the civil war. I thought it quite shocking that forty years after the war, some deputies in Leinster House would still be continuing the fight. He pointed out, however, that the Americans were still fighting their civil war more than one hundred years later and that we had made considerable progress.

I could not agree with him when I saw the extent of the patronage in operation in relation to all sorts of public appointments, and saw the endorsement of this policy by all the leading politicians.

Shortly after I took up duty in Leinster House, there was a debate about a booklet called *Facts about Ireland*, produced by the Department of Foreign Affairs and sent to Irish embassies all over the world. Fine Gael objected strongly to what its members saw as an attempt to play down the role of Michael Collins in the establishment of the state and to promote the role of de Valera. Cork Fine Gael veteran John L. Sullivan, friend and companion of Collins, was furious at the publication and demanded that the matter be rectified in a new publication.

For some strange reason, Donogh O'Malley was sent in to defend the government case, and he immediately disarmed the Fine Gael veteran by telling the House that Collins was one of his great heroes, an admission which must have stunned some of the older members of Fianna Fáil. He promised to ensure that in any future edition of the book, Collins would get his proper acknowledgement.

I was very impressed, and O'Malley immediately went into my diary as a politician to be cultivated. But he undid some of the good work by going on to philosophise about the need to recognise that in war the spoils went to the victors and that in a contest for appointment to a position in the state, 'other things being equal', a Fianna Fáil applicant would always get the job over a Fine Gael supporter. It was quite a shocking philosophy and I thought to myself that it would take a bolt of lightening from Heaven to strike this place to restore a sense of order.

The following day, I was drinking coffee in the Dáil restaurant with my colleagues when we were joined by James Dillon, Jim Gibbons and Sean Dunne, an ebullient Labour man who once led a hunger march in support of farm labourers, walking in his bare feet through the streets of Rathdrum, County

Wicklow. In later life, he bought an old Mercedes car but was too embarrassed to let his constituents in Ballyfermot see the car, so he used park it outside the constituency and go into the area by bus. He was one of the finest raconteurs I ever met and he and Gibbons and Pat Lindsay enlivened many an afternoon when the Dáil was in recess, as each tried to tell a better story than the other.

On the afternoon I speak about, the conversation turned to the debate of the previous night over *Facts about Ireland*. None of the politicians appeared to see anything wrong with the position outlined by O'Malley that the spoils went to the victors. Again, I was shocked at the seeming acceptance of a philosophy which would require ambitious young people to pursue the most successful political party in order to secure promotion. I made the mistake of blurting out my belief that it would take a bolt from Heaven to strike the place to restore reality. Instantly, all three politicians rounded on me for daring to suggest that there might be something rotten in the state of affairs.

Over the years afterwards, I watched in dismay as all the young barristers rushed off to join Fianna Fáil, not out of conviction about the party's political philosophy but because they believed it was the best way to secure a rung on the ladder of promotion which might eventually lead to the Supreme Court.

In terms of political philosophy, I soon discovered that there was little difference between any of the three political parties. I became convinced that you could move one-third to one-half of the deputies of any of the parties across the House to the other side and that they would be there for several months before they would recognise the change.

Declan Costello and some of his friends in Fine Gael, including Garret FitzGerald, tried to introduce a new and more radical social element into the political debate by producing a splendid booklet, *Towards a Just Society*. With some difficulty, it was accepted by Fine Gael as the basis for future development, even though the more traditional members of the party had problems with some of its concepts. Declan himself spent many years promoting his policy, often suffering setbacks and disillusionment but in the end being proved right. When he eventually left the political scene, his departure was one of the great losses for Irish parliamentary life. Like George Colley, whose unfortunate early demise followed an apparently simple operation in a London hospital, both left their parties with gaps which could never be filled.

Jack Lynch's success in winning the Fianna Fáil leadership was another development which gave hope to a new and more idealistic approach to politics. I formed a strong attachment to him which persisted through his career until his death. I often said in later years that there were few political leaders to whom I would have given allegiance. Seán Lemass was my first hero, followed by Jack Lynch. Others who won my support and my affection included Paddy Hillery, Garret FitzGerald, Des O'Malley, John Hume and Seamus Mallon. I would have liked to be able to include Charlie Haughey in the list, since there was much that was likeable about him but every time I decided to make a move towards him, I found he was involved in some activity of a questionable nature, so that I could never rid myself of the belief that there was a basic flaw in his character. With the passage of the years and as he went further up the ladder of success, his undesirable traits became all the more obvious, until I became convinced that he was a considerable threat to the democratic process. All that time, of course, the Fianna Fáil party suffered. The party, which my parents had helped to get off the ground in Laois–Offaly in the 1920s was now an organisation bordering on corruption, whose main supporters were no longer the small shopkeepers and farmers of rural Ireland but the builders and hucksters who had their grubby little hands in the national till and whose success depended on the level of financial support they were prepared to give to Fianna Fáil. As George Colley and

I agreed when the support group, Taca, was set up, 'Nobody gives £100 to sit down to a Fianna Fáil dinner unless they expect to get £200 in return.'

Dr Paddy Hillery should have been the natural successor to Jack Lynch as leader of Fianna Fáil, but a series of circumstances, including his own reluctance to put himself forward for the office, effectively ruined his chances. A medical doctor from Clare, he had drawn attention to his potential at an early stage under Dev. He was a successful Minister for Education and an even more impressive Minister for Foreign Affairs. He did not attract general attention in the party, however, until he seized the microphone at the Fianna Fáil Ard Fheis in 1971, in the aftermath of the Arms Crisis. As hordes of Kevin Boland supporters chanted, 'We want Boland', Hillery, to the delight of Jack Lynch supporters, shouted back, 'You can have Boland, but you cannot have Fianna Fáil.' It was the emergence of a new, more forceful Hillery, on whom Jack Lynch relied for support for the rest of his career.

If Lynch wanted Hillery to succeed him, however – and there is little doubt that he did – he should have kept him closer to his side. Instead, he sent him off to Brussels as European Commissioner for a term. When Hillery returned to Ireland, Lynch allowed his name to be put forward for the office of President, when there were other possible candidates. At the then comparatively young age of 53 years, Paddy Hillery found himself lost in the stifling atmosphere of Áras an Uachtaráin. Worse still, when he completed his seven-year term, Haughey, then Taoiseach, put forward Hillery's name for a second term. Under Mary Robinson and Mary McAleese, the remit for President was widened considerably, but in Hillery's time, it remained very restrictive and he spent fourteen of the best years of his life in a ceremonial role when he could have given so much more to his country and to his party. On the other hand, it could be said that his holding of the office helped to restore the prestige of the presidency which had been badly damaged by the row between Liam Cosgrave's government and Cearbhall Ó Dálaigh over the insult to the President by Paddy Donegan, the Minister for Defence.

From the 1970s onwards, however, the great hope was Garret FitzGerald, who was going to reform our society, restore trust and confidence in the political institutions and wipe out corruption at all levels. It was a huge task but he was brimful of energy, boundless enthusiasm and total commitment. The one thing he lacked, and which became more obvious as the pressures of office increased, was the ability to delegate responsibility and to keep his finger out of every pie. He made an excellent appointment in Peter Prendergast as National Organiser. Prendergast hit the local organisation in the party like a tornado, getting rid of old fogies who had held the party back for years, and replacing them with new, young representatives who were to play a major role in building up FitzGerald's Fine Gael. But otherwise Garret showed himself to be a poor administrator, inclined to get bogged down in detail and allowing cabinet meetings, at which he presided, to drag on interminably until individual ministers became completely bored by the proceedings.

John Boland, who had been one of Garret's most active supporters, now became one of his most severe critics. A notably impatient man, Boland could not tolerate the extent to which debate at cabinet was allowed. It was a return to the old days of Dev who would allow debate on particular issues to be extended to the point where ministers were totally exhausted and, as Lemass told me, they would have agreed to anything to get out of the cabinet room. So, when Dev said, 'I take it, gentlemen, we are all agreed,' there was not a murmur of disapproval.

One area on which FitzGerald spent an exceptional amount of time and which eventually yielded results was Northern Ireland. Margaret Thatcher had humiliated him by her rude rejection of the possible solutions put forward by the Forum on

Peace and Reconciliation. Her anxiety to make amends led to her acceptance of a formula put forward by FitzGerald in what became known as the Anglo–Irish Agreement and which formed the basis for all the subsequent developments towards peace in Northern Ireland. Haughey claimed that FitzGerald was about to sell out the national aspiration to Irish unity. Ignoring FitzGerald's intention to secure for the first time a direct input by the Irish government into the running of affairs in Northern Ireland, Haughey attempted to undermine the agreement. He sent Brian Lenihan to the US to lobby the influential Irish-American group of Ted Kennedy, Daniel Patrick Moynihan and Hugh Carey to oppose the agreement. Fortunately, they saw through Haughey's almost treasonable activity and rejected his efforts. The agreement succeeded and Haughey and his successors in Fianna Fáil used it as a stepping stone to later developments The Anglo-Irish Agreement will stand in history as FitzGerald's greatest achievement.

On his constitutional crusade, however, Garret was less successful and the objective was gradually lost sight of in the demands made on his time and energies by less important matters. His obsession with detail worried many of his friends and caused the downfall of his government at the 1981 budget over a stupid proposal to tax children's shoes. It was sad to see him down on one knee pleading with Jim Kemmy in the Dáil chamber to support the government proposals when it was quite clear to any objective observer that Kemmy could not vote for the proposal. Meanwhile, another Independent, Sean Loftus, who might have been persuaded to vote with the government, was sitting two seats away and nobody asked him for his vote. When Garret held a press conference later in the day to explain why children's shoes could not be excluded from the general proposal to tax women's shoes because some women wore children's sizes, it became clear that he was being completely impractical and that an office which for so many years he had struggled so hard to

A group of journalists surrounding Princess Grace at a press reception in the Shelbourne Hotel, Dublin. The journalists include Vincent Corcoran (on her right), George Leech, Michael Mills, Paddy Glendon, Tony Gallagher, Tony Kelly, Cathal O'Shannon and Sam Edgar. In the background on the left of the picture is Frankie Byrne.

Jack and Maureen Lynch seen praying at morning Mass in August 1968, at the Roman Catholic cathedral in Bombay. Jack Lynch was on an unofficial visit to the city and met Irish nuns and priests working there. He was the first Taoiseach to have made a tour of the Far East. Kneeling behind the Lynchs are journalists Joe Fahy, Arthur Noonan, Wesley Boyd and Michael Mills.

L-R: Michael Mills, Chris Glennon, a White House official, Dick Walsh, Liam O'Neill, Seán Duignan and Kevin Healy.

Garret FitzGerald and party in Georgia during Dr FitzGerald's visit in December 1976. *L-R:* Mike Burns, Denis Kennedy, a Russian interpreter, Joan FitzGerald, Garret FitzGerald, Sean Cantwell, Michael Mills and an Irish Embassy official.

L-R: Vincent Jennings, Michael Mills, Tim Pat Coogan, Dr Eamon de Valera and Sean Ward. The portrait is by Pat Phelan.

President Paddy Hillery with Michael Mills on the occasion of his appointment as Ombudsman. Also in the picture is the Danish Ombudsman, Dr Neils Holm..

A presentation to Gay Byrne by the Publicity Club of Ireland at
Fitzpatrick's Hotel, Killiney Castle.

Michael Mills meets King Juan Carlos at an Ombudsman conference in Madrid.

The Ombudsman presents the annual report with Frank Goodman, senior investigator, and Dermot Curran, first director of the office.

Michael Mills with cartoonist Flann O'Riain at the opening of an exhibition of cartoons at Kitty O'Sheas pub.

Michael Mills with his friend Liam Flynn, art editor, *The Irish Press*, at a journalists' golf outing at Royal Dublin Golf Club.

As Ombudsman.

obtain was being almost recklessly discarded in pursuit of an absurd idea. It was a grave disappointment to so many people who had hoped for much more. In the circumstances, he was lucky to get a second bite at the cherry when Haughey's government collapsed in 1982. It was during that second period in office that the Anglo-Irish Agreement came into being. It was and will be remembered as the high point in the life of a sincere and hardworking politician who was also a genuinely good man.

One of FitzGerald's biggest mistakes was in allowing his government to be pressurised by the pro-life lobby into introducing a referendum on abortion. His excuse was that he feared he would be outmanoeuvred by Haughey if he refused the pro-life lobby and Haughey accepted. Haughey would then be able to accuse the government of being in favour of abortion.

Once it had been decided to promote a constitutional referendum, the question arose as to the wording of the resolution. Various formulae were considered and, again, Haughey outmanoeuvred FitzGerald. Bishop Brendan Comiskey told me that he had a phone call from Haughey asking him to call out to Kinsealy. He arrived early one morning and was met by Haughey in his dressing gown at the front door. Haughey produced a piece of paper and slipped it into his breast pocket, saying, 'This should be of interest to your friends.' Comiskey brought the wording on the slip of paper to his colleagues at the next bishops' meeting. They immediately endorsed it.

FitzGerald's government also endorsed it but, two days later, the Attorney General, Peter Sutherland, concluded that the wording was dangerously ambiguous and warned against putting it before the people in a referendum campaign. The warning was too late and, much as FitzGerald struggled to recover ground, the campaign was turned into a debate about the wording rather than about the issue of abortion. Thousands of people who were opposed to abortion could not vote for a change in the constitution which they knew was dangerously worded and could lead to endless trouble in the future.

I was on a radio programme on RTÉ with William Binchy, a strong pro-life activist, shortly before the referendum day. I pointed out that the wording of the resolution was highly dangerous, that it would lead to court challenges in certain circumstances and that it should not be proceeded with. I appealed to Cardinal Cahal Daly as head of the Catholic Church in Ireland to bring an end to the widely divisive debate now being conducted around the country. I said it was splitting many families, all of whom were opposed to abortion but some of whom could not bring themselves to supporting this dangerous wording. If there was need for a referendum, which many of us doubted, let a consensus be found on a new formula.

On the following Sunday, I was attacked from the altar by a local curate in my parish church as a 'neo-Protestant' who should keep his mouth shut about moral issues. The parish priest, give him his due, apologised the following Sunday for his curate's remarks.

The campaign proceeded, the referendum was carried and, a few years later, we had the 'X' case, with all its ramifications, arising directly from the wording of the amendment. The problem continues to the present day and no political party is going to run the risk of trying to resolve it.

⌘ ⌘ ⌘

Sean Lemass was easily the most impressive politician of my generation. He lived in Dev's shadow most of his life, waiting impatiently for the chance, which de Valera was slow to give him, to take charge. It was only in 1959 that Dev reluctantly let go the leadership and went as President to Áras an Uachtaráin, leaving Lemass in charge of Fianna Fáil and of the government. Ironically, despite the widespread regard in which he was held, Lemass twice led Fianna Fáil into a general election and failed each time to secure an overall majority. Jack Lynch, who succeeded him, was less able but was far more popular and won a majority on his first attempt.

It was one of the tragedies of Irish politics that Lemass had only seven years at the top before declining health forced him to step down. However, in that short time, he had given a new impetus to Ireland's drive towards self-confidence, setting our eyes towards Europe and a new perspective on industrial development. The pity was that Dev should have hung on to power in the 1950s when Lemass was at the height of his powers and was capable of giving a dynamic push to a struggling nation. The first programme for economic expansion, which he launched with the assistance of Dr T. K. Whitaker, lifted the despondency of the younger generation especially and set new targets for the economy.

When he retired, I wrote to him expressing my regret on behalf of my generation that we had not more time to appreciate his qualities of leadership. Within a year, I was conducting a series of interviews with him which gave me further insights into the extent of his talents and his extraordinary memory of dates and events, stretching back for more than half a century. He had a gruff personality which some people found intimidating and he had little time for small talk. If there was business to be done, his philosophy was to get down to it straightaway. I did a series of thirteen interviews with him in his office at Leinster House, recording them on a poor-quality tape machine which was quite likely to break down at any time. In fact, it broke down twice and I came away with nothing on the tape. The first time, I asked him to repeat the interview, to which he readily agreed, but the second time I was too embarrassed and wrote up the material from memory. With one or two minor amendments, he agreed with my presentation. He never looked at a note or consulted a document during the entire period of the interviews. In fact, many times he was well into his responses before I had completed the question. It was a delightful experience to work with him and my only regret was that the publication of the interviews was rushed at the end before I had proper time to evaluate and prepare the material. The editor was impatient to get the material published as quickly as possible. The only difficulty that Sean Lemass had during the interviews was in talking about the civil war and, particularly, about the killing of his brother, Noel, in the Dublin mountains. At that point, he paused and said, 'If you don't mind, we will not talk any further about that period. Terrible things were done on both sides.'

He remained entirely aloof from politics for the remainder of his life, only reluctantly giving an interview to RTÉ at the time of the Arms Crisis of 1970, indicating that he believed that Jack Lynch had no alternative but to take the action he did in sacking two of his ministers, one of whom was Lemass's son-in-law, Charlie Haughey.

⌘　　⌘　　⌘

Haughey was the most talented politician of his time. He was extremely bright, capable of grasping the most complex and detailed briefings with a minimum of effort and presenting the most impressive case to his peers, at home or abroad, without fear of challenge. But, unlike Lemass, he was conceited to an unusual degree and he was very greedy for the good things of life. Lemass had little interest in fine wines or sophisticated dishes, whereas Haughey made it his business to learn about wines and good food. Lemass had no great interest in money, provided he could play poker with his friends when he felt like it. Haughey, on the other hand, was interested in all the trappings of wealth – an impressive house, considerable land and horses and, above all, unlimited money. He did not give the impression of being insecure but his need for all these attributes of wealth and prestige obviously indicated a dependence which was almost childlike. He loved showing off his paintings and his sculptures, some of which were impressive, and he liked doing a tour of the grounds around Kinsealy with visitors, paying special attention to the lake and the swans.

His childish interest in style and pomp manifested itself in the early days when he used to turn up at meetings of the hunt, dressed in a bowler hat and riding boots, much to the amusement of Dubliners who regarded it as a classic example of beggars on horseback. Most people are not born to wear bowler hats and Haughey was one of them. He succeeded only in being a figure of fun.

When he got down off his high horse, he was a very likeable person, witty and with a great sense of fun, often at the expense of some other person in the company. As he got richer and more powerful, his character changed. Where one time he would talk with affection of his humbler background and of his mother, he now avoided conversation which might indicate a gentler side to his character.

One of the features of his house at Kinsealy that he used to liked to show off was the specially designed bar, with counter and beer taps, where visitors would be invited to sample the products. Over the bar was a wooden harp presented to him by the prisoners in Long Kesh, and over the entrance door was a plaque commemorating the signatories of the proclamation of 1916. One cynical Northern journalist pretended not to recognise the names and suggested they might be the names of former barmen. He was one of a group of journalists invited out to the house by Haughey to be briefed on the presentation he intended making that weekend in Brussels to the Council of Ministers of the European Union. A couple of years later, at a similar gathering in Copenhagen, which he was attending shortly before he left office following his defeat in the general election of 1982, he complained bitterly about the unfairness of the Irish system which had given him a higher vote than any of his contemporaries in Europe, and yet he was leaving office while they were continuing to hold power.

Ironically, for a man who loved horses, his conference was held in a converted warehouse on the docks in Copenhagen, once used to house horses. The Danes, who had done a remarkable job in restoring these older buildings along the dockside, had failed completely to rid the walls of the pungent and unpleasant odour of horse manure. Haughey was so angry at the unfairness of life that I doubt if he was aware of the smell.

The arrival in 1979 of Haughey as leader of Fianna Fáil gave the political climbers an opportunity they could not afford to miss. For the expenditure of a comparatively small amount of money in their terms, they could get access to the corridors of power. They seized the chance and they could be seen parading around Leinster House with all the arrogance and ignorance of the newly arrived rich. They turned up in droves at the party's ard fheiseanna and whooped with delight at every silly utterance from the platform. They went delirious when Haughey told them that if there was oil off the coast, Fianna Fáil would find it and bring it ashore.

When he told them that it was time to tighten their belts because we were spending too much money, they nodded their heads in admiration at the wisdom of the man, who proceeded himself to seek out his friends to ask them for more money to enable him to continue with the lifestyle to which he had become accustomed. Anybody who questioned the source of his wealth or the purity of his intentions was regarded as an enemy of the state whose republican credentials were open to serious question. It was a time of deceit and duplicity when good people like my mother became so disillusioned that they ceased to vote at all.

⌘   ⌘   ⌘

There were, of course, events that occurred over the years that raised hopes of new thinking, and the development of fresh policies that gave hope of genuine change. One of them was the emergence in the late 1960s of a new drive by the Labour Party to attract support with a policy document promising that the 1970s would be socialist. It was prepared by party secretary Brendan Halligan, a bright young man who had worked his way through Trinity College and was now trying to attract a new type of recruit to the Labour Party. The trouble was that the new policies were not explained fully or properly to the existing members who went on radio and television to make it clear that they had not a clue what the whole thing was about.

But they did attract a new and more academic type of candidate. One of the brightest was Conor Cruise O'Brien, a brilliant writer and commentator whose courage and insight helped to throw light into many dark corners of Irish society. The trouble was that he was too often right in his analyses and people got tired of his being proven to be right. Eventually, many neutral supporters who had been attracted to him turned against him. They decided he was too clever by half. David Thornley, a first-class lecturer in politics and influential television presenter, became another shining light and was joined by Justin Keating, an equally prominent university lecturer and television performer. But Thornley lacked the stamina needed for the long haul in politics. Tedious political debate in the Dáil and long-winded arguments in the party rooms absorbed his energies and killed his interest. He turned to drink and it was heartbreaking in his later years to see him, still a comparatively young man, wandering around the European Parliament in Strasbourg with nobody to talk to and even his friends slipping quietly out of his way.

The most interesting of the new group of Labour deputies was a man with no academic background whatever. Frank Cluskey was a former Dublin butcher with a marvellous sense of humour and a razor-sharp wit, making him the best of company.

He fought the demon drink and won for long periods until the loneliness of life in Strasbourg during the sittings of the European Parliament led him to think that a drink or two would not do him much harm. He died from cancer at a comparatively early age.

⌘ ⌘ ⌘

Liam Cosgrave was a most unassuming individual. It was not force of personality that secured him the leadership of Fine Gael but the fact that he was the son of W. T. Cosgrave, the first leader of the modem state. He was not widely popular among the voters but he had an innate sense of decency which won him universal respect. His word was his bond – once given, it would never be broken.

Many in the parliamentary party at Leinster House grew impatient with his old style approach to politics. They looked to the younger blood in the party to shake up Fine Gael. Garret FitzGerald and Declan Costello were obvious choices for a new and more enterprising party. Cosgrave watched the advances of these younger men with much suspicion and a strong belief that they were seeking to replace him.

His suspicion manifested itself publicly and embarrassingly at an annual conference of the party in Cork where he referred to his enemies within the party as 'mongrel foxes' who would be hunted down by the hounds. It required considerable restraint by the supporters of FitzGerald and Costello to avoid a walk-out from the conference.

A similar outburst occurred five years later near the end of his days as leader when he became angry at journalists whom he described as 'blow ins' who were attacking the Coalition Government on isssues of human rights. The blow-ins were not named but, he suggested, they should 'blow out or blow up'. Again, the general reaction was shock and embarrassment.

He led a comparatively successful government from 1973 to 1977 during which he negotiated the Sunningdale agreement, which, if it had been given a chance might have avoided years of strife in Northern Ireland. This achievement, however, tends to be obscured by the memory of a Taoiseach walking across the Dáil to vote with the Opposition against his own government's Contraceptives Bill.

In May 1970 he initiated one of the most dramatic developments in modern Irish politics when he went privately to the then Taoiseach, Jack Lynch, and challenged him with information about the involvement of a number of his ministers in an attempt to bring guns illegally into the state. Uncertain how to handle the situation, Cosgrave had first shown the Garda information to his friend, Ned Murphy, political correspondent of the *Sunday Independent*, whose editor, Hector Legge, declined to publish the material for fear of libel action by the people against whom the allegations were made. In the end, Cosgrave consulted with his closest colleagues, some of whom favoured blowing the Fianna Fáil Government out of the water. However, the majority felt that the welfare of the state should be the first consideration and that Cosgrave should go and talk to Lynch.

Cosgrave had earlier that day hinted in the Dáil that a major story was about to break. Jack Lynch had just announced the departure from government of the Minister for Justice, Micheál Ó Moráin, following an embarrassing outburst by him earlier in the week at a dinner of the Canadian Bar Association. Cosgrave asked the Taoiseach if this was 'the tip of the iceberg'. Lynch, unaware of the information in Cosgrave's possession, replied that he did not know what the deputy was talking about. None of the journalists who heard the exchange pursued the matter until they were called from their beds in the early hours of the following morning with the news that Haughey and Blaney had been sacked.

He was never a man for ostentation or pomposity and he

hated publicity. He never tried to influence anybody to write favourable comment about him and he was equally considerate towards journalists who wrote kind and unkind things about him. One journalist, who would not have been regarded as a supporter but who was sent by his newspaper to cover many of Cosgrave's activities, very often attracted his concern because of a serious disability. Cosgrave would frequently enquire about his welfare from other journalists.

Cosgrave took defeat in the 1977 election just as he had taken the victories, with almost stoic acceptance. On the day that Jack Lynch was elected Taoiseach, Liam Cosgrave sat, a lonely figure, in the furthest of the backbench Opposition seats, eyes firmly fixed on the desk in front of him. He never made another political contribution.

Before his election as Taoiseach, he agreed to do an interview with me at his office in Dún Laoghaire. When I arrived there, I found a number of other journalists, mainly from British newspapers and the BBC, waiting for interviews. He suggested we slip away in his car and do the interview in the car park of a supermarket just off the main street in the town. I hopped into the passenger seat of his old car parked outside the office and attempted to close the door behind me, but the door handle came off in my hand. Embarrassed, I tried to hide it under the seat but he told me not to bother, just to push it back into its place. I did so and immediately forgot about the faulty handle until we had completed the interview and I went to get out of the car back at his office. Again, the door handle came off in my hand and I was left standing on the footpath with the handle in my hand, trying to pretend that this was a normal occurrence in interviewing people who were about to be elected leaders of their country and who would never again have to drive their own cars. He was not in the least way put out by the occurrence. It was a trivial matter of no consequence.

⌘ ⌘ ⌘

After 1969, and despite the Arms Crisis in the following year, Jack Lynch's stock continued to rise. He had succeeded in winning an impressive victory for Fianna Fáil in the general election and his popularity with the general public was manifest. He made some bad enemies with his sacking of Haughey and Blaney but he also gained many supporters by his decisive action in that regard. The Fianna Fáil party was, however, badly divided on the whole affair. Diehard republicans started to come out of the woodwork to be joined by others who had never been in Northern Ireland but felt it was time to manifest their emotions in outbursts over a few pints in their local pub.

The majority of Fianna Fáil TDs were on Lynch's side but they retained a certain sympathy for their former ministerial colleagues and justified their ambivalence with the suggestion that 'their hearts were in the right place' and that it was perfectly understandable that they would seek to help out their Northern brethren.

The trial of Haughey, Blaney, Jim Kelly, John Kelly and Albert Luykx for attempting to import arms illegally into the state should have clarified the situation. Instead, it merely helped to confuse the matter further. Jim Kelly's disclosure of information about the secret Army directive should have been anticipated by the legal team who advised the Government on its decision to prosecute the defendants for attempting to import arms illegally, but it may have been hoped that the disappearance of the directive from Army files during the court hearing would cast sufficient doubts on Kelly's story to discredit his claim. Unfortunately, if that was the case, the Government had not allowed for Michael Hefferon's support of Kelly's claim, backed up by the statement he had recorded at the time.

However, there was no real analysis of these details and they were gradually lost sight of until the commencement of the hearings of the Public Accounts Committee into the disappearance of the £100,000 Government fund for the relief of distress in Northern Ireland. By that time, however, the public had become tired of the whole complex story and wanted to get back to normal living, so that much of the material disclosed to the Committee went either unreported or unread.

Within Fianna Fáil, however, the affair continued to eat into the heart of the party and the hostile attitudes of the supporters of Lynch on the one side and Blaney, Haughey and Kevin Boland on the other, continued to fester. The matter came to a head when the Opposition put down a motion in the Dáil expressing 'no confidence' in the Minister for Defence, Jim Gibbons. The Government countered with a motion of confidence in the members of the Government, who, of course, included Jim Gibbons.

Blaney did not have to face the embarrassment of supporting the motion as a Government deputy; he had already been expelled from the party. But Haughey and Boland were forced to make a decision. The reporters on the press bench watched the drama unfold below them in the Dáil chamber. If Haughey voted confidence in Gibbons, he would be publicly implying that Gibbons had told the truth in the Arms Trial. The judge had said that Haughey and Gibbons could not both be telling the truth; one of them had to be telling lies. At the time, we did not know the extent to which Haughey was prepared to humiliate himself in order to hang on to his membership of Fianna Fáil and use his position, however lowly it might be, to precipitate himself eventually to power.

We had temporarily forgotten Kevin Boland until he stood up from his seat in the back benches, came down the steps, walked across the floor of the Dáil and out through the door behind the Ceann Comhairle's chair. It took a second or two for us to realise that, rather than vote confidence in Lynch and his Government, Boland had opted to walk out of the Dáil and out of Fianna Fáil. Haughey, as might be expected, walked into the 'yes' lobby behind Lynch.

I felt like standing up and cheering Boland's display of integrity, no matter how ill-thought-out and impetuous it was. It represented one man's declaration of principle. Shortly afterwards, Boland attempted to set up a new party, Aontacht Éireann, but never got it off the ground; in a short time, it was dead and its founder ceased to have any further influence in Irish politics.

Lynch was now embarked on a programme aimed at achieving Ireland's entry into the European Community, which was duly achieved. He made several visits to European capitals to advance our case and the attendant publicity helped to boost his stock still further. He was now completely in control of Fianna Fáil and he had around him a team of ministers totally loyal to him. He had no longer to worry about Haughey, Blaney or Boland coming up behind him. The departure to Brussels of Paddy Hillery as Ireland's first European Commissioner was a major loss from the cabinet but Lynch felt it was necessary to make a strong pro-Community statement by appointing one of his best ministers, even though he would miss Hillery's close advice in the years ahead.

Haughey embarked on a rehabilitation programme and got himself selected as one of five vice-presidents of Fianna Fáil, a post which enabled him to travel around the country ingratiating himself with local party supporters. He cultivated press reporters and journalists of all shades. He even attended as guest of honour the annual dinner of the Leinster House press gallery, held at Dublin Airport. I was deputed to look after his welfare and took the trouble to learn his favourite wine. Two bottles of the vintage went down to the gallery's expense – an expense it could ill afford – but nothing was too good for the great man. The dinner began with the chairman of the gallery, Michael Barber, attempting to say the Grace before Meals. Whether it was the result of nervousness or excitement, he began what he thought was the prayer before meals, but turned out to be an Act of Contrition. Instead of 'Bless us, O Lord and these, thy gifts' what emerged was 'O my God, I am heartily sorry for all my sins.'

At that stage, he was drowned in an outburst of laughter, realised his error and got back on to the proper prayer. It broke the ice and enabled Haughey to drop his aloof manner and become a little more human. Since the Arms Trial, he had become suspicious of other people and had lost most of the warmth and humanity which he had exhibited previously. It was not easy to find subjects to discuss with him. The most obvious one, politics, was a minefield. The evening went pleasantly enough until, near the end, some people had drunk a little too much and two elderly pressmen began to argue over the Civil War. One was a well-known Blueshirt, the other a self-proclaimed republican. Insults like 'Ballyseedy' and the '77 Martyrs' were flung across the table as the two protagonists got up from their seats to edge closer to one another. I turned to Haughey to advise him not to worry about the situation, that it was all playacting, but he was not there. At the first hint of trouble, he had pushed back his seat and disappeared into the darkness of Dublin Airport, without a word of thanks for the meal or the fine wine. The surprising thing was that nobody thought his behaviour odd. He was Charles J. Haughey and he was entitled to behave differently from other people.

Relations between politicians and journalists had not been formalised at this stage. Individual politicians like Haughey set up their own contacts with press people, using them whenever it suited their agenda, but the arrival of a proper communications system with regular briefings for journalists had to await the arrival of the Coalition Government of Liam Cosgrave in 1973. There was a Government Information Service in operation previously under Pádraig Ó hAnnracháin, a witty civil servant with a great gift for mimicry and story-telling. He and Lord Carrington got on famously when Carrington accompanied

Margaret Thatcher to Dublin for discussions with Haughey on Northern Ireland and Anglo–Irish relations generally. But Pádraig had no authority to give regular press briefings or to inform journalists of the agenda for government meetings. He regarded his task as mainly answering queries from journalists and fobbing off questions which could be embarrassing for ministers. He was close to Haughey all his life and, when he retired, Haughey brought him back to advise him on political issues and to keep an eye out for his enemies.

⌘   ⌘   ⌘

The Coalition Government of 1973 was formed after Fine Gael and Labour gained a narrow victory over Fianna Fáil. Jack Lynch, in a remarkable performance, succeeded in improving Fianna Fáil's vote over the 1969 total, but was beaten through the transfer of votes between Fine Gael and Labour after the leaders of the two parties, Tom O'Higgins and Brendan Corish, made a pre-election pact based on a 14-point plan. They could have secured power in 1969 but in a major pre-election speech at that time, Corish ruled out any pact with Fine Gael. The result was that votes failed to transfer between the two parties.

Corish came from a political family in Wexford. He was a very likeable man, affable and modest. He found it a little difficult to handle the motley group of deputies who came onto the Labour benches after the 1969 election and included Conor Cruise O'Brien, David Thornley and Justin Keating. He was more at home with the old-time Labour men like Michael Pat Murphy and Jim Tully, but he managed to run a reasonably successful operation in the four years of the Coalition Government. Liam Cosgrave and he got on very well together, which was a big help to the cohesion of the government. On one occasion, they were both missing for some hours and nobody could locate them. Eventually it was discovered that they had locked themselves in Cosgrave's office to watch the horse racing at Cheltenham without interruption.

Conor Cruise O'Brien, as Minister for Posts and Telegraphs in the 1973 Government, was given charge of communications generally and became responsible for briefing Muiris MacConghail as Government Press Secretary on the general outlines of the agenda for government meetings. This was a completely new development which removed much of the secrecy surrounding cabinet sessions and made the public more aware of the nature of government operations. Muiris would then come to the political correspondents' room in Leinster House, outline the details of his briefing with O'Brien and answer follow-up questions from the correspondents. If we were unhappy with the nature of his replies, we would ask him to go back to Government Buildings and get us more information. Other journalists working at Leinster House who were not invited to these sessions commenced to criticise them and to suggest that they were mere exercises in political propaganda. However, the political correspondents had been starved for years of a proper information service and had relied entirely on the friendship or goodwill of individual ministers, for which a price had to be paid later in a less critical analysis than might be justified in the case of an individual minister. So, we found the new system to be an invaluable addition to the communications system, paving the way eventually for the Freedom of Information Act, brought in by Eithne FitzGerald.

Muiris, unfortunately, paid the penalty of being too successful at his job. Senior Fianna Fáil people, of whom more might have been expected, let it be known that he would suffer when Fianna Fáil returned to power. I had tried to warn him when he left RTÉ to take up the job of head of the Government Information Service that he might find many doors in RTÉ shut on his return. He was to learn that politics can be a very nasty business and that a price would have to be paid for making a political statement. He was one of the best people ever to work in the communications business, and a fund of knowledge on all matters concerned with broadcasting. He returned to RTÉ when the Coalition Government left office in 1977 but he was no longer on the ladder of promotion in RTÉ.

The Cosgrave Government had to contend with an early financial problem created by an oil crisis on a global scale. Difficult decisions had to be taken which aroused a hostile reaction among the public, but, generally, the management of the budget situation was reasonably successful. One of the commitments made by the parties in their pre-election agreement was to introduce a tax on wealth. The tax introduced was a fairly liberal item, starting at wealth and property above £250,000, or the equivalent of about €2 million in today's values. Very few people were in danger of being affected but many thought that it was only a matter of time till the tax was extended to affect their property. Some influential commentators, such as Gay Byrne, John Healy and Bruce Arnold, started a campaign to undermine the proposals, and managed to attract considerable attention. At the same time, a satirical programme on RTÉ commenced to ridicule members of the government by presenting caricatures of the principals, such as 'Richie Ruin' (Richie Ryan, the Minister for Finance) and 'Mein Führer' (the Taoiseach, Liam Cosgrave). It was a funny programme and a highly successful attempt at political satire which owed its origins mainly to the pen of Frank Hall, a most entertaining performer. However, the programme did considerable damage to the Coalition Government and ceased when Fianna Fáil got back into power in 1977. The claim was that there were no characters in the new government who lent themselves to caricature

The Coalition Government itself created many of its own problems, notably the attack on President Ó Dálaigh by the Minister for Defence, Paddy Donegan. The President had decided to submit to the courts the question of the constitutionality of a new piece of legislation introduced by the Government to deal with the growing problem of the Provisional IRA. Donegan called the President a 'thundering disgrace'. He had too much drink taken at the time but he sobered up quickly when the furore started, and offered his resignation to Cosgrave. Cosgrave made the mistake of not accepting Donegan's resignation and compounded the mistake by not going personally to Áras an Uachtaráin to apologise. Instead, he used the telephone to make contact with the President, which further annoyed Ó Dálaigh who eventually felt that he had no option but to resign from the office.

More embarrassment was to be created for the Government when it tried to bring in a Bill to legalise the sale of contraceptives. Liam Cosgrave gave no indication of his attitude to the Bill, beyond emphasising to his cabinet colleagues that there would be a free vote on it. They assumed that the free vote was to accommodate some of his deputies who might have difficulty in conscience in supporting the Bill. They never thought that he was referring to himself as having a free vote, since nobody in government had ever voted against government legislation. Paddy Cooney, the Minister for Justice, and his cabinet colleagues watched in disbelief as the Taoiseach left his seat in the Dáil, and walked up the steps into the Opposition lobby, followed closely by the Minister for Education, Richard Burke. It was a severe blow, from which the Government never fully recovered. Trust could not be restored. In terms of public perception, the damage was widespread. A government that could not be relied upon to vote for its own legislation could scarcely be expected to run the affairs of the nation with any great degree of credibility.

In time, however, the memory of the contraceptives debacle faded and the Government's image began to be restored. The achievement of the Sunningdale Agreement early in the period of the Coalition Government created a good stock of credits and gave a considerable boost to Liam Cosgrave's leadership. He had taken over the reins of office in 1973 with no great public confidence surrounding him. Within a year, he was at Sunningdale, chairing with Ted Heath a conference which promised to bring lasting peace to Northern Ireland. At the end of several days of hard bargaining with the Northern parties, a very convincing series of proposals emerged. There was one glaring weakness, though. The Irish side had made too many demands, including the creation of a Council of Ireland. It was a proposal around which the enemies of the agreement gathered in the following days, slowly eroding the air of optimism that surrounded the close of the conference. The smile of success on the faces of Liam Cosgrave and John Hume as they left Sunningdale was gradually replaced with expressions of frustration and anger as the so-called 'workers' strike' closed down Northern Ireland, and the British Government watched helplessly as all business was brought to a halt. We asked Liam Cosgrave how he would have dealt with the problem. 'I would have hosed them off the streets,' he said, grimly. But the workers' resistance succeeded.

Sunningdale was destroyed, only to be revived years later in a new format and with stronger hopes of success under new leaders, and with John Hume still leading the nationalist cause, to remain one of the most outstanding politicians of all time in Ireland.

⌘   ⌘   ⌘

In 1975, I got an invitation from the US State Department to visit the US for four weeks. I opted for visits to Washington, Chapel Hill University in North Carolina, New Orleans, Colorado Springs, San Francisco, Chicago and New York. I was asked to give a talk on the situation in Northern Ireland to a group of Rotarians in Colorado Springs.

Chapel Hill I found to be a most interesting, if highly conservative, institution, where the word 'socialism' was distinctly suspect. Having entered into debate on European politics with a number of members of staff, I found that they were most anxious to pigeon-hole me for political definition. I was very interested at the time in experiments that were taking place in Spain and Portugal in the development of democratic socialism. I spoke to them about these developments and they decided immediately that I was a socialist.

A couple of days later, I found that discussion about democratic socialism was less acceptable with some people. I had a meeting arranged with a group of newspaper editors in Raleigh. They questioned me about political developments in Europe. Again, I had just referred to the situation in Spain and Portugal when one of the editors looked at his watch and reminded me that I had a bus to catch back to Chapel Hill. The discussion was over and I realised that 'socialism' was a dangerous word to be throwing around in parts of America.

In Colorado Springs, I had an audience of about 600 people for my talk on the situation in Northern Ireland. I decided to concentrate my fire on the activities of the Provisional IRA and the growing series of atrocities they were committing in the name of the Irish people. While claiming to be the defenders of the Catholic minority, its members were engaged in widespread bombing of civilian targets, resulting in the deaths of hundreds of innocent men, women and children. I told them of the bombing of Claudy and Coleraine and 'bloody Friday' in Belfast, and a long list of other depravities. From the time they planted their first bomb in the electricity board office in Belfast in 1971, killing two young girls and permanently maiming twelve others, I had come to the conclusion that they were a greater scourge to my country than the infamous Black and Tans.

Like most American audiences, this one was not very interested in events occurring thousands of miles away, but I received a polite reception. One member of the audience, however, with an obvious Irish background, told me that I did not know what I was talking about and, if he had time, he would like to give me a lesson in Irish history. He reminded me of the Irish-American barman I had met in New York a year earlier who made a subscription to the IRA collection box every time it was passed around. When I tried to point out that his sub might be going to buy explosives or ammunition to kill a fellow Irishman, a third party drew me aside and advised me not to be wasting my time. The barman, he told me, was third-generation Irish-American. He had never been to Ireland in his life but religiously donated ten dollars each time the collection box went around for 'the cause'.

I went on to San Francisco where I was sitting in my hotel room one afternoon, writing an article for *The Irish Press*, when I heard a shot down the street, followed by a wailing of police sirens. I went down the street to find out what was causing the excitement. I discovered that President Gerald Ford was visiting the city and, just as he was leaving the St Francis Hotel, a block away from my location, somebody in the crowd had fired a shot at him. By the time I arrived on the scene, most of excitement had died down and both the President and the would-be assassin had been whisked away. The shooter was a young woman called Sarah Jane Moore, who had placed herself in the crowd on the corner across the road from the entrance to the St Francis. Fortunately, somebody standing near her spotted the gun and struck her arm just as she was about to fire. Were it not for the vigilant observer, she could have done damage. The bullet struck the wall of the hotel entrance, leaving a jagged piece of masonry as an indicator of its flight. It was about seven feet up from the ground, indicating that it was much closer to causing damage than the reports suggested. Miss Moore, it was learned later, craved publicity and had used the occasion for the purpose. Her ambition was realised when her picture appeared on the cover of *Time* magazine a week later.

⌘ ⌘ ⌘

Despite the many blunders made by the Coalition during their four years of government, they still appeared to have sufficient credits in hand to approach the 1977 general election with some confidence. Fianna Fáil, fearing a second and more convincing defeat than in 1973, laid plans to ensure a public recovery. Surveys conducted during the 1973 campaign had shown considerable interest in the problems of domestic rates and growing taxation on cars. With a reckless disregard for the state of the country's finances, the party embarked on a programme of promises to abolish domestic rates and motor taxation and provide a gift of £1,000 for each first-time buyer of a new house. It was a totally irresponsible preparation for the general election but it had a massive influence on the outcome. Fine Gael deputy Gerry L'Estrange told me that, having read the list of promises and totted up the benefits for himself, he had reached a figure of £2,000 before studying the small print. 'If, on top of that, I were a first-time house buyer, I would have no option but to vote for Fianna Fáil. If the Irish people vote for the Fianna Fáil promises, Fine Gael will be hammered.' I had to agree with him but I still did not believe the electorate would be conned into voting for a list of promises which threatened to bankrupt the country. Over the next ten years, the country ran deeper and deeper into debt until the World Bank seemed likely to take over the running of our finances.

In the first two years of Jack Lynch's new Government, a massive debt of £6 billion was built up which doubled to £12 billion under Haughey's leadership between 1979 and 1981. When Garret FitzGerald took over, the debt rose over the next four years to £24 billion, but it declined somewhat as a percentage of Gross National Product, which is the criterion used by international financiers in assessing the financial stability of a country. When Haughey returned to power in 1986, he got great credit for reducing the national debt and bringing spending into line, but he was merely correcting a problem that he and Fianna Fáil were largely responsible for creating. My boss, Vivion de Valera, could not understand why I was so sceptical of his party's promises. I told him that if they were implemented, they would bankrupt the country. His father, I told him, would turn in his grave at the notion of Fianna Fáil offering the people bribes for their votes. 'What are you going to promise next time,' I asked him, 'radial tyres and windscreen wipers?'

The result of Fianna Fáil's largesse in the 1977 election was a return for the party of 84 seats in the Dáil, the largest return in the history of the party and a majority of 20 seats over the combined opposition. Nobody had predicted an outcome of this sort, least of all Fianna Fáil whose main anxiety was to avoid suffering too heavy a defeat in the election. Most of the commentators had been influenced in their predictions by a constituency revision carried out by the Coalition Government which increased considerably the number of three-seat constituencies and appeared to make it impossible for any political party ever again to secure an overall majority. I had a chat with Jack Lynch in the course of the campaign in which I told him that the outcome of a personal survey I had carried out suggested that a swing of 3 per cent to Fianna Fáil from Fine Gael would put Fianna Fáil in with a good chance of victory. He did not take my predictions very seriously. 'Michael,' he said, 'if you conducted a similar survey in some other part of the country, you would probably find an entirely different result. All I can say is that the crowds coming to my meetings are bigger than in 1973.' He did not disclose to me that Fianna Fáil had conducted a series of opinion polls over the course of the campaign which showed the party well on the way to victory with a percentage share of more than 50 per cent. One poll showed support running as high as 56 per cent. The lowest figure was above 50 per cent, and that is the way the election turned out. Only one Fianna Fáil official,

Jack Carroll, consistently predicted that the party would win 77 seats. In fact, when the counting reached 77, there was a sort of domino effect, and the total went on to 84.

On the Sunday before the election, a group of political commentators was brought on RTÉ to discuss the possible outcome of the election. We hedged our bets as far as possible until Sean Duignan, who could not resist a good storyline, talked of meeting an old political observer during the week who assured him that if Fianna Fáil won the election, it would be like Lazarus coming back from the dead. It was a good line and it was left hanging round our necks for the next week. We were recalled the following Sunday to be reminded of Lazarus, at which Duignan commented that if Lazarus had returned from the dead, he had brought back many of his friends with him. All of us burst into laughter, but behind the laughing I knew that our reputation as reasonably accurate forecasters of political events was in tatters.

5 Pursuit over the Border

In 1977, Jack Lynch led Fianna Fáil back into government with the biggest majority in the history of the state. He admitted on the night of victory that the majority was too large and could create future problems. His fear was justified in the ensuing years. The backbenchers, many of whom knew that they were unlikely to hold onto their seats in another election, became restless. Any evidence of vulnerability on the part of the leadership was in danger of being exploited.

Two years later, in 1979, an event occurred which shocked the nation and shattered any hope that Jack Lynch had of a reasonably secure period of government. The Provisional IRA murdered Lord Mountbatten in a bomb attack on his boat just outside the harbour at Mullaghmore in County Sligo.

Jack Lynch was on holidays in Spain at the time with his wife, Maureen. He returned home to attend the ceremony at Baldonnell Airport, on the removal of Lord Mountbatten's body by air to London. Two days later, he attended the funeral service in Westminster Cathedral, on behalf of the Irish Government. He was deeply embarrassed by the failure of the Irish security forces to protect a man who was close to the British royal family and who was still regarded by the British public as a hero; he was at his most vulnerable

It was not surprising that Lynch was subjected to extreme pressure by the British Prime Minister, Margaret Thatcher. She wanted concessions in the security area. He conceded something which had previously been refused by Liam Cosgrave's government – permission for British helicopters to cross the border for a limited distance in cases of 'hot pursuit'. The new security arrangement apparently permitted the establishment of an air corridor of ten kilometres – five on either side of the border – to be used by helicopters or light aircraft from Northern Ireland or the Republic in cases of hot pursuit of suspected terrorists. Permission for the over-flights could come only from an officer of the rank of brigadier general or higher.

Rumours began to circulate in political circles within days that there had been a stepping-up in the security arrangements between the two sides of the border. Nobody would confirm, however, that there had been any change or what the nature of the change might be. Having considered all the possible security changes that might have occurred, it seemed to me that the most likely development was not on the ground but in the air. Already, there had been a considerable improvement in co-operation on the ground between the security forces on both sides of the border; the most up-to-date techniques had been put in place for immediate communication between the Garda Síochána and the RUC. Hundreds of thousands of pounds had been spent on radio-telephonic links to ensure quick closing-off of the border in cases of emergency.

A change in security in the air could only mean the establishment of an air corridor to ensure continuous surveillance of suspected terrorists fleeing across the border after an attack on targets in Northern Ireland. Obviously, similar surveillance would apply in the event of an attack by the UVF on a target in the Republic.

I tried out my theory of an air corridor by way of a casual question to a senior civil servant a few days later. He was stunned by the question. Before he could collect himself, he said, 'My God, where did you hear that?' and instantly switched the subject; but he had confirmed for me the accuracy of my assumption. Armed with this confirmation, I went looking for some guidance on the extent of the corridor. I learned, after a series of trial-and-error questions that the distance was 10. Having been educated in a system that recorded distances in miles rather than kilometres, I assumed that the distance was 10 miles, instead of 10 kilometres.

My story in *The Irish Press* the following day was followed by instant denials from all government sources. Members of the Fianna Fáil parliamentary party were suspicious, however, and deputy Bill Loughnane of Clare asked the Taoiseach, Jack Lynch, if any change had occurred. Mr Lynch assured him that there had been no change in the sovereignty exercised by the state over our air space. This was true, insofar as we still retained the sovereign right to permit or deny access to our air space, but it did not clear up the mystery as to where *The Irish Press* story had come from, and whether it had any basis in fact. The story was given additional emphasis by the publication in the *Daily Telegraph* a day or two later of similar material, with the extent of the corridor being stated as 10 km which indicated to me that the source of the *Telegraph* story was the British Government or the Northern Ireland Office since there was a complete blanket on information from the Irish side. No Irish newspaper, apart from *The Irish Press*, carried the story, but they all carried a denial by government sources that there was any truth in the matter. Within the Fianna Fáil parliamentary party, however, there remained the suspicion that it might be true, despite Jack Lynch's claim that the sovereignty of our air space remained unaffected. For myself, I considered that the change was a minor development in terms of cross-border co-operation, particularly in the light of the heinous killing of Lord Mountbatten and a young local boy at Mullaghmore; but an indication of public feeling was brought home to me shortly afterwards when my 90-year-old mother sought my reassurance that the story could not possibly be true. The idea of British helicopters being allowed to enter Irish air space was for her completely unacceptable. The fact that we were quite happy to use British helicopters on mercy missions to assist in air-sea rescues or to take injured people to hospital was not seen as a good counterargument.

Shortly after this, came two by-elections in Jack Lynch's own territory of County Cork. The forecasts were that Fianna Fáil would win both elections, but as I watched Jack Lynch's final rally in Cork City on the eve of the elections, it seemed to me that his extraordinary personal appeal to voters, which had seen him achieve such historic success in the 1977 general election, had diminished greatly. Gone was the old enthusiasm of the crowds; in its place was a dull apathy which, I suggested to some of my colleagues, did not bode well for Fianna Fáil's prospects in the by-elections.

The results confirmed my predictions. By that time, we were thousands of miles away in Washington on a visit by the Taoiseach to meet Irish-American industrialists in a number of US cities. He took the results of the Cork by-elections very badly. It was obvious at an impromptu press conference for Irish political journalists accompanying him on his US trip that he was profoundly shaken by the results, particularly as they were from his own county where he would have expected the old loyalties to be maintained. The harsh realities of political life were beginning to close in.

But, this was a minor matter compared to an event that was to take place the following day at the National Press Club in Washington where Jack Lynch had been invited to deliver a speech and to take questions from US journalists afterwards. He concluded his speech and answered a number of routine questions. The function was almost over and most of the journalists had put away their notebooks when the Washington correspondent of *The Irish Times*, Sean Cronin, asked what new arrangements had been made about the over-flying of our national territory.

Lynch, still suffering, possibly, from jet-lag, and relaxed after a couple of glasses of wine with his lunch, was quite unprepared for the question. He said that the regulations under the Air Navigation Acts remained unchanged. Unfortunately for himself, he did not stop there; he added the significant phrase 'except in one slight respect'. There was an audible gasp of 'Oh, my God' from one of the Irish civil servants on the top table. I already had my notebook out of my pocket and was writing furiously away as Lynch went on to explain about the slight change in the regulations.

I sent over a story from Washington to *The Irish Press* that night, to the effect that the Taoiseach had confirmed my story of a couple of months previously about the setting up of an air corridor on the border. Lynch did not, of course, describe it as such, but his admission of a change in the regulations governing over-flights led to an explosion in the Fianna Fáil parliamentary party. Deputy Bill Loughnane, who had asked questions about the matter when *The Irish Press* story was first published, now called Jack Lynch 'a liar'.

Lynch was furious. The group of Irish journalists travelling with him on his US trip were practically frozen out as he wrestled with the internal party problems threatening to undermine his leadership. Even Maureen Lynch found it difficult to give us her usual welcoming 'good morning' as we boarded the special vice-presidential air-force plane which had been placed at Lynch's disposal. We left Washington and travelled via Chicago and New Orleans to Houston in Texas, pursued by messages from home about the repercussions in the Fianna Fáil party. By the time we arrived in Houston, Lynch had made up his mind to fire Bill Loughnane from the parliamentary party. It may have been the only option available to him to restore his authority but it was a highly risky undertaking to engage in from a distance of 5,000 miles. He decided to ask George Colley, who was acting leader in his absence, to put down a motion at the next parliamentary party meeting for the removal of the whip from Loughnane.

We were attending a rodeo on a ranch in Houston when he made the fateful call to Colley. There were only two telephones available on the ranch, one an outdoor kiosk which was being used by Dick Walsh of *The Irish Times*, and a second inside the ranch-house, which was being used by me to send copy to *The Irish Press*. I was talking away on the phone in a small room when a burly FBI man knocked peremptorily on the door. 'Sir,' he said, 'we want that phone for your Prime Minister.'

'Mr Lynch can have the phone whenever he arrives here,' I said. 'But in the meantime I intend to complete my conversation with my office in Dublin.'

He left in a huff. I completed my call and was leaving the building when I met Jack Lynch coming in. He was clearly in a bad mood. I greeted him but he barely nodded in reply before going inside to make what I believed was a call to Dublin to set in motion the wheels for Bill Loughnane's dismissal. Two days later, we learned that his efforts had failed. The parliamentary party refused to support George Colley's motion, especially after deputy Vivion de Valera had opposed it on the grounds that Bill Loughnane's original question to Jack Lynch about cross-border over-flights had not been properly answered, and after Loughnane had softened to some extent his original position.

Nevertheless, it represented a public challenge to his authority. Even his decision to remove two ministers from his government at the time of the Arms Crisis in 1970 had not been questioned; but now a backbench deputy was, apparently, to go undisciplined after calling the Taoiseach 'a liar'. Deputy Loughnane went even further in the following days by calling for Lynch's resignation.

Lynch could easily have fought off any challenge to his leadership but it seems that he had already some months earlier discussed with his wife, Maureen, the possibility of taking early retirement at the beginning of 1980. He now moved that date forward by a few months. His frustration at the inability or unwillingness of the parliamentary party to deal with Bill Loughnane boiled over, however, shortly before the end of the US trip when he gave a press conference at his New York hotel to the Irish journalists who had accompanied him on the trip.

He was answering a general question about the internal row in Fianna Fáil when he stopped in mid-sentence and pointed a finger at me, saying, 'You, Michael, started all this with your ten-mile air corridor.' I started to protest but he interrupted me. 'If I say ten kilometres, you'll say ten miles, and if I say ten miles, you'll say ten kilometres,' he said. At this point, Chris Glennon of the *Irish Independent* tried to pour oil on the troubled waters only to draw Jack Lynch's attention away from me on to himself. At that stage, the Government Press Secretary, Frank Dunlop, intervened to bring the press conference to a close.

Lynch came back to Dublin to face mounting rebellion in the parliamentary party. He could have faced it down and would almost certainly have defeated any challenge to his leadership, but, having decided to go, he stuck by his decision, being convinced by his closest advisors that George Colley, whom he trusted, would succeed him in any electoral contest.

The advice was bad, however, as any of the political correspondents could have told him at any time in the preceding months. For more than a year, we had been conducting regular polls among ourselves as to the likely outcome of a leadership contest between George Colley and Charles Haughey. In every one of them, Haughey came out on top.

The only person who ever asked me for an opinion on the outcome was Mr Haughey himself. I told him that our estimates gave him 45–46 votes. He was somewhat disappointed, as he told me his own estimate put him at more than 50 votes, but then, he said, 45 votes would be a victory in any case. Up to the end, Colley's supporters continued to express absolute confidence in the outcome. I tried to explain to one of his aides that they were being misled and that some deputies were obviously promising their votes to both men, but they were not prepared to listen and, in any case, it was too late. Haughey won by 44 votes to 38.

The over-flight concession continued to operate under Haughey, despite the vociferous opposition by his supporters to the arrangement when Lynch was in power. As far as I know, it continued to operate under Albert Reynolds and remains in force down to the present time.

The circumstances of Jack Lynch's departure as leader were sad and disillusioning. He deserved better of a party he had brought to such extraordinary electoral success. Not only did he not succeed in having his choice of successor endorsed by the party, who chose instead Lynch's old enemy, Charlie Haughey, but in the succeeding years, Fianna Fáil adopted a Stalin-type purge to erase Lynch's name from the records. His name was not mentioned at Fianna Fáil's Árd Fheis and his photo was not carried in the Árd Fheis booklet. But, the wheel has now turned full circle and Fianna Fáil has been attempting to present the current leader, Bertie Ahern, as 'the new Jack Lynch'. The irony of this development is not lost on Jack Lynch's friends who recall that Bertie Ahern was Haughey's protégé.

Lynch's problem may have arisen from the fact that he was always something of an outsider in the eyes of diehard republicans. He had no national record and none of his family could claim to have had a national record, unlike Neil Blaney, whose family could point to a long republican association in Donegal, or Charlie Haughey, whose record was less obvious but who had no difficulty in putting on the required mantle in 1969.

⌘　　⌘　　⌘

The publication by *The Irish Press* of the political obituary of Charles J. Haughey years before his departure from the political scene was a major faux pas. The publication, in January 1983, came after the revelation of the tapping of the phones of two journalists and at the end of the most serious attempt up to that time to get rid of Haughey, by his opponents in Fianna Fáil. The attempt seemed likely to succeed after Haughey indicated to a meeting of his parliamentary colleagues that he would not be hounded out of office by the media but would make up his mind in his own good time. This was taken as a clear signal of his intention to go in the immediate future.

Throughout a parliamentary party meeting on 27 January 1983, RTÉ's current affairs programme was broadcasting dramatic accounts of Haughey sitting up in his office in Leinster House, drafting his letter of resignation. Down in the political correspondents' room, nobody believed a word of it. We knew Haughey and we knew that he was not a man who would easily depart the leadership, having spent so much time and energy to get there. If he went, he would be pushed; he would not voluntarily hand on power to somebody else.

In the newspaper offices in Middle Abbey Street and on Burgh Quay, however, the editorial staffs were glued to television and could not understand why they were not getting corroborative stories from their political correspondents. In frustration, the editor of *The Irish Press* insisted on sending up to Leinster House a journalist with no experience of political reporting, to find evidence to support the RTÉ story. Inevitably, he became embroiled in the media frenzy around Leinster House that night and became convinced that Haughey was about to resign. He succeeded in conveying this conviction to the editor's office in Burgh Quay, where Tim Pat Coogan, had been torn for hours between sticking with his political correspondent's less dramatic story and running the risk of being beaten by an *Irish Independent* scoop. In the end, he decided to take a risk and run with the dramatic story of Haughey's resignation.

I was completely unaware of the discussions taking place at editorial level in Burgh Quay, or that consideration was being given to the notion of publishing Haughey's political obituary in the morning paper. If anybody had mentioned such a possibility to me, I would have argued vehemently against it. It was with considerable shock therefore that I heard the first news of the obituary on RTÉ's 'What it says in the papers' at eight o'clock the following morning. I had left Leinster House at 12.30 that morning after a final check with the Fianna Fáil whip, Bertie Ahern, who confirmed the story I had earlier sent to *The Irish Press* that Haughey had gone home to consider his position and would make up his mind in a day or two. In fact, he had gone to the Olympia Theatre to hear the final stages of a concert being given by his friends, the Fureys.

I rang the news editor to let him know the up-to-the-minute position and to confirm that my 'holding' story, of Haughey going home to consider his position, should stand. That story appeared on the front page of *The Irish Press* that morning but, unfortunately, it was superseded by the dramatic impact of the political obituary. It was several days later before I could unravel the sequence of events that had led to the publication. By that time, Haughey had changed his mind completely about resigning, as I predicted he would do on the morning of the publication of the obituary. I said to my wife, 'Whatever possibility there was of Haughey resigning has now gone. He is not going to allow *The Irish Press* to decide his future. He will now dig in his heels and stay in power.'

Knowing Haughey's long memory for actions hostile to his welfare, the editorial staff started to look for ways of spreading the blame for their serious misjudgment. Suggestions were made that an assistant editor had made a wrong call but they were quickly withdrawn when the individual threatened legal action. It was then suggested that the error resulted from bad advice from the 'political staff', which was sufficiently vague to embrace everybody working at Leinster House that night, including the political correspondent, who was as amazed as the rest of the country to hear the news next day.

6 Ombudsman

In October 1983, I was in Berlin, writing a background story about the proposed visit to Ireland of the German President when I got a telephone call to my hotel early one morning from Dublin, from the Minister for the Public Service, John Boland. He told me he had been asked by the Government to offer me the job of Ireland's first national Ombudsman. I expressed surprise at the offer. I was very flattered to be chosen but told him frankly that I knew nothing about the job.

He said, 'Welcome to the club; nobody else knows anything about it either.'

I said that I would love to take the job if I thought I could do it, but while I had studied from a distance the great work being done by Ombudsmen in other parts of the world, I was basically quite ignorant of the procedures and would need to study them at length.

He said that that could easily be arranged and he had already made plans to bring to Ireland for a short visit the Danish Ombudsman, Dr Neils Holm, who could be a great help in setting up the new office. 'Anyway,' he said, 'you don't have to make an instant decision. Ring me when you get back to Dublin at the weekend.' In the meantime, he would send the relevant papers about the job to the Irish Embassy in Bonn if I could arrange a suitable meeting place to pick them up from an official. The only place I could think of as a meeting place was the Catholic Cathedral in Cologne where I expected to visit the next day. It was a most unsuitable place for an appointment, with its hundreds of visitors walking up and down the aisles but, as it turned out, the official and I discovered one another quite easily and he handed over to me the file on the Office of the Ombudsman.

John Boland had warned me that I must not discuss the matter with any of my colleagues in case I should turn down the offer, as the next in line would be compromised if he learned that he was only second choice. So, I read the file in secret over the next day or two and rang my wife from a public phone in an Irish pub in Berlin the following evening. I told her of the Government's offer and that I was trying to make up my mind what to do. I was now in my mid-fifties and the notion of taking up a new appointment in a totally strange environment was quite intimidating. She asked, 'What do you want to do?'

I said that I would love to take the job if I thought I could do it.

'Well, then,' she said, 'take it. You know you can do it.'

I told her that I was certain of one thing: if I said 'no' I would never be able to forgive myself. 'Right,' I said, 'I will ring John Boland tomorrow to accept the offer.' I rang him that evening and told him that I would take the job provided that there was no objection from other party leaders, especially Charles Haughey. He said that he had discussed the matter with the other party leaders and all had agreed to my appointment. In that case, I said, go ahead with the arrangements and thank Garret FitzGerald and the Government for their trust in me.

I learned later that one of the reasons that Haughey agreed to my appointment was that it would end my position as Political Editor in *The Irish Press*. When I met him some time later, he wished me well in my new office but I became aware before long that he did not really wish the Office of Ombudsman well. While the Ombudsman Act had been introduced in 1979 under his Government, he had no serious intention of bringing the Act into operation and it was not until the arrival of Garret FitzGerald's Government that the Act was activated, in 1983, to come into operation on 1 January, 1984.

In the meantime, John Boland wanted to announce my appointment as Ireland's first national Ombudsman. After my return from Germany, we talked about the matter and I pointed out to him that I would have to inform my editor of my impending departure from *The Irish Press*. So, on the evening of John Boland's announcement, I was photographed at my desk in *The Irish Press*, writing up the story of my appointment.

It was agreed that I would work out my notice in the paper and that I would officially take up duty in the Ombudsman's Office in January 1984. Before I actually took up duty, I was faced with my first complaint, which turned out to be a most complex and long-drawn-out affair. I was coming out of Leinster House one afternoon when a lady passing on her bike hopped off and came across to me. 'You are the answer to my prayers,' she greeted me and proceeded to tell me of her failure over many years to obtain a social welfare benefit to which she felt she was entitled. She had been in touch with seven ministers and twelve Dáil deputies. All had been unable to help her and her last hope was my office.

I asked the new members of my staff who had been appointed and were in an office at the top of Harcourt Street to have a look at the case and see if we could help. We sent for the files and found that she had been turned down for benefits because she did not have sufficient stamps. We asked Social Welfare to look at the case again and to give it to a new officer who had not seen it before and who might adopt a more positive approach to the question of why she *should* get her benefits rather than why she should not.

This new officer looked at the question of credits rather than stamps and found, under an old and little-used regulation, that she should be entitled to eighteen months' credits as a married woman returning to employment at one stage in her career.

She was paid her benefits and everything appeared to be ending well until she wrote to thank me for my help and asked would I now get her the true value of the back money paid to her. As she rightly pointed out, £1 paid to her in 1984 would buy far less for her than would £1 paid to her in 1970. I agreed with her and began a long and hard-fought battle with various departments and particularly with the Department of Finance to secure her the necessary compensation. The Department of Social Welfare was willing to make an ex gratia payment of a small sum but I was anxious to secure an amount equal to the inflationary value of the money over the years, and to secure it as her right rather than as an ex gratia payment.

All my efforts were in vain and eventually I was driven to the preparation of a special report to the Dáil. Before presenting the report to the Dáil, however, I decided to write to a small group of ministers, pointing out what was at issue and how necessary it was that the Government introduce regulations to ensure that persons who had been wrongfully deprived of their benefits over a period of time should be paid an amount equal to the inflationary pressures on the money over the period.

The Minister for Finance told me that I was exceeding my authority but I pointed out to him the section in the Act which enabled me if I were unhappy with a particular settlement to seek further redress. In the end, the Department of Finance conceded my case and it was agreed that in future there would be a statutory right to compensation where benefits had been wrongfully withheld over a certain period.

It was one of our first major achievements in a period when several government departments were making our work difficult by creating delays in making files available and, in some cases, declining to answer queries. It was only after I threatened these people with the possibility of court action for contempt that all of them fell into line. The new and younger breed of civil servant coming on stream changed the outlook of the civil service completely. There was a fresh willingness to co-operate and a desire to provide a more open and transparent approach to public enquiry.

The health boards were the last to come on board. Chief executives had ruled their domains with almost dictatorial powers for so long that they found it hard to tolerate any intrusion by the Ombudsman's Office into their affairs. Some local authorities adopted a similar stance.

Many senior civil servants with whom I had been friendly and with whom I had often enjoyed a drink now avoided me. In order to avoid embarrassment, I also ceased going into my favourite pub, Doheny and Nesbitt's. Indeed, my life became largely reclusive and I found my social life confined to the company of my office friends, and our discussions related mainly to aspects of the more complex cases we were examining.

Many of these cases became subject to major analyses and to concentrated investigations of the files. One case which gave us enormous difficulty related to a young lady suffering from a rare blood disease. She had been successfully treated in the US but was refused payment for the treatment by her local health board. The Health Board's case was that a team of medical experts had recommended to the Board that the necessary treatment could be carried out at home and there was no need for her to travel abroad for treatment. One of my senior investigators went through the files meticulously and could find no cause for disagreement with the Board's case. I had an instinct that something was wrong and went through the file for several days. After six examinations of the files, I had to admit defeat, even though I continued to have a niggling feeling that something was suspicious.

In a last desperate effort, I went through the file a seventh time and found the missing link. The medical experts, who, it was claimed, had recommended that treatment be provided at home, could not have met on the day the decision was claimed to have been taken because the expert most involved in the case was attending another meeting in a different location on the same day. The Board admitted its misleading information but made no apology.

I found it more and more difficult to get health boards to admit to their mistakes. They ignored my recommendations in some cases until I threatened to make a special report to the Oireachtas, naming the offenders. This procedure always brought them around, though in some cases they fought right down to the line. One CEO, whom I called to my office to warn him that I would report the case to the Oireachtas within ten days if he did not accept my recommendation or advance a reasonable case in his defence, thumped the table and told me that he was not going to be intimidated. I told him that he was at liberty to leave the room but I had no intention of entering into a shouting match with him. His legal advisor, who was with him, calmed him down and we went through the case line by line until, in the end, he had to admit that my office had taken every factor into account and that the recommendation had been made only after the most painstaking procedures. He eventually accepted the recommendation with bad grace. Ten years later, a lady came up to me at Dublin Airport to thank me for the work we had done on the case, which had resulted in her daughter getting proper medical treatment in the following years.

For the most part, complainants were very grateful for the work we carried out on their behalf but one case on which we spent an enormous amount of time disappointed us. A lady wrote to us about her failure to obtain a deserted wife's benefit after her husband went off to England and left her on her own. To make a claim for the benefit, a form must be filled in which contains a very confusing question: 'Did your husband leave of his own volition?' The answer to that question has to be 'yes' if the wife is to be deemed eligible to receive the benefit. However, my complainant, being a simple woman, consulted her local TD, whom I shall call 'Murphy'. Murphy, being a wise man, advised her to write in 'No' to the question, which meant that she had practically no chance of getting the benefit, since the answer suggested that she had put him out.

She was refused the benefit and her husband went on to divorce her and marry another woman in England. Then he died and she applied for the widow's pension but the Department of Social Welfare, under the law on domicile, decided that his second wife was his widow for the purposes of the Act. So, she ended up with nothing.

We carried out an investigation of the case, found in favour of his Irish widow and recommended that she be given the deserted wife's benefit back to the date when she had first made the application, and that the payment should take into account the inflationary effects on the money over the years. In all, she got over £30,000 but we never got a word of thanks from her.

Some years later, I was in the town where the lady lived and met the gentleman who had first brought the case to my attention. I mentioned to him that we had got the case resolved and that she had got a very substantial amount of money but that we had never heard from her since to express a word of thanks. 'Why would she write to your office,' my friend said, 'when Murphy was the first to tell her the good news? He told her he had eventually secured her rights after years of fighting the Department. As far as she was concerned, Murphy was responsible for her good luck. Your office had nothing at all to do with it.'

'Well,' I said, 'she died last year and now she knows the truth,' and I moved away from him. He called me back, saying, 'You're forgetting something.'

'What's that?' I asked. He said that Murphy had died the previous year also.

⌘　　⌘　　⌘

In the first year, we handled more than 2,000 cases and in our second year, we got almost 5,500 complaints which made exceptional demands of our staff of twenty-five members. Much of the increase was accounted for by the addition to our remit of complaints about telephone accounts. Every telephone user in the country felt that they were being overcharged. I could not prove that they were being overcharged, but neither could Telecom Éireann prove that they were not. So, I decided on a formula of striking a balanced judgment on the evidence and, after considerable argument, Telecom accepted my judgment as the best solution to a very complex problem, while acknowledging that the only way the problem could be properly resolved was by a new and detailed system of billing. This would make telephone subscribers aware that their phone was being used in some instances by members of their family to make long-distance calls to various parts of the world, to their boyfriends or their girlfriends, or in some cases to sex-chat lines, usually in the US.

About two years after taking on responsibility for examining telephone complaints, Michael Smurfit, the Chairman of Telecom, went before one of the public accounts committees to complain that my office was obliging Telecom to spend £25 million on the installation of new equipment to provide detailed information in regard to telephone accounts. Somebody had fed him misleading information. His company was preparing to spend £25 million on new equipment but the decision had been taken long before my office had become involved. The expenditure would undoubtedly help to meet my recommendation for detailed accounts for subscribers but it was merely in keeping with good practice in accounting, as was the custom in other parts of the world.

Soon afterwards, there was a call to my office from the Department of Finance, seeking information on the procedure to be followed to remove Telecom from my remit. My office informed the enquirer of the procedure but pointed out that, of course, the removal of the remit could occur only after a decision by the Oireachtas. The requirement that the Oireachtas would have to be informed, and would have to pass a motion to that effect, immediately put an end to the proposal which had obviously been reached with a certain amount of conspiring behind the scenes. The naiveté of the Department of Finance enquirer gave us much cause for amusement, while it also made us aware of the extent of the hostility out there towards the Office of the Ombudsman.

⌘ ⌘ ⌘

Ombudsmen, like all public servants, love to travel. They also take themselves very seriously and they like to listen to themselves talking, so there are regular conferences in different parts of the world. One of the first conferences I attended was in Stockholm where my director, Dermot Curran, and I were the new boys and were treated as such. We made good friends with our neighbours in the UK, particularly the Welsh and Scottish representatives, and also with the Ombudsmen from the Nordic countries, but some of the larger countries adopted a superior attitude to their smaller-country colleagues. A distinctly pompous air crept into the debates at regular intervals, particularly when the Ombudsmen from those countries arrived with entourages of six and seven underlings to laugh at their jokes or applaud their more pompous utterances. I found it quite offensive and noticed that some of my colleagues from Asia, with whom I had become friendly, were also offended by it. One morning, I stopped my good friend from Sri Lanka and suggested that we should do something about it. He agreed and said that he would back me up. I demurred on the grounds that I was only the new kid on the block whereas he, as a former member of the Supreme Court in his own country and with a great deal of experience as Ombudsman, had the necessary authority to make the criticism.

Somewhat reluctantly, he took on the task and, at the end of the first session that morning, he told the conference that he and others had been struck by the apparent arrogance of some of the members at the conference. He suggested that it would be a good exercise for every Ombudsman, on getting out of bed in the morning, to go on their knees and pray to God for humility. I clapped enthusiastically but found that I was the only one applauding his speech. Neither he nor I was greeted with any great warmth for the rest of the conference.

⌘ ⌘ ⌘

As the months went by and we became more experienced in our procedures, we were able to speed up the process. We were also involved in developing an entirely new computerised system which made it easier to track down cases, analyse the progress being made and limit considerably the amount of paper work. I now had a staff of twenty investigators, including four senior investigators, and the work of the Office was proceeding quite smoothly. But always I knew that a change of government was a possibility and that the support of the Taoiseach, Garret FitzGerald, and Minister for the Public Service, John Boland, would not be a constant in the equation. As I feared, C. J. Haughey returned to power in 1986, and my nightmare began shortly after.

At the time, I was trying desperately to persuade successive Ministers for Social Affairs to recognise limited rights, at least, for old age pensioners who did not have enough stamps to qualify for a full pension to get access to a pro-rata pension for the amount of stamps they had accumulated during their years of work. To get a full pension, you needed an average of twenty stamps a year. Some of my clients had fifteen and sixteen stamps; some even had eighteen and nineteen stamps. But under the regulations they could not qualify. With the nightmare of severe cutbacks in the funding of my office, I had to forego my lobbying on this issue for the time being, but I was hopeful of getting back to it when the political situation changed. In the end, it was Michael Woods, the Fianna Fáil Minister for Social Welfare, who brought in the necessary change in the regulations to allow for pro-rata pensions for persons with less than the required average of twenty stamps. It was a huge breakthrough for thousands of pensioners who had been frustrated for many years.

⌘ ⌘ ⌘

Shortly after I had been appointed Ombudsman and before the Office of the Ombudsman opened officially, the Department of the Public Service introduced a supplementary estimate for the Office of a sum of £8,000 for the payment of legal fees. It was a nominal sum which might have been expected to pass through the Dáil without question. However, Mr Haughey, who was leader of the Opposition at the time, immediately rose to question the purpose of the money. Patrick Cooney, who introduced the estimate in the absence of his colleague, the Minister for the Public Service, John Boland, explained that the money was a nominal amount to cover legal fees, for which provision had not been made in the original estimate. (In fact, the entire £8,000 was absorbed in the payment of a single account for legal advice a few months later).

Haughey said that he would allow the estimate through on this occasion but that the Government should not expect such an easy passage in the future. It was the first public display by him of hostility towards the Ombudsman's Office. It was not noticed widely in the Dáil, but for me it was an indication of what might happen if he ever got back into government again.

For the next two years, my time was taken up completely with the hundreds of problems associated with setting up a new office which had the overwhelming support of the public but was treated with alarm and suspicion by many people in the public service, particularly the more senior members. I was blessed with an extraordinarily dedicated staff, headed up by the Director, Dermot Curran, who worked long hours to get the Office working successfully in dealing with some thousands of complaints. These complaints had been building up for years and had failed to find a solution until the Ombudsman's Office was set up.

I met Haughey only rarely in that time. One of the few occasions was at the funeral of the great folksinger, Luke Kelly, when, as I was getting into my car outside the church in Santry, he came over to speak to me. Without asking me directly, he indicated a general interest in how the Ombudsman's Office was doing. I told him of the difficulties I was encountering, especially with senior civil servants. It was a brief conversation and he manifested no concern for my problems, nor did I expect him to, but I felt that at least his questions indicated a more friendly attitude towards the Office, which could be helpful in the future.

Three years later, Fianna Fáil came back into power with C. J. Haughey as Taoiseach. He set out immediately to remedy the financial situation which was quite desperate after a series of disastrous government decisions since 1977 and Fianna Fáil's implementation of its irresponsible election promises. By 1979, a national debt of £6 billion had been run up. Haughey took over leadership from Jack Lynch in that year and, over the next two years, doubled the national debt to £12 billion. In the next four years, Garret FitzGerald's Government doubled that figure again to £24 billion. There was little doubt that the country was close to bankruptcy.

Haughey immediately introduced a series of the most severe cutbacks which averaged out for most departments at about 12 per cent, except in some cases, such as the medical research department set up only three years previously under my good friend Dr Ivo Drury, which he closed down completely. In the case of the Ombudsman's Office, the cut was 20 per cent. Of my budget of £500,000, a sum of £100,000 was removed.

It was clear to my Director, Dermot Curran, and to me that this would have disastrous effects on the Office and that the only way the situation could be met was by letting five of our staff of twenty investigators go. We started to make enquiries as to where they might be accommodated without losing their status or their salary. Fortunately, the Department of Social Welfare had vacancies at a similar grade and could accommodate our five investigators, but we had to make up our minds quickly or the vacancies in Social Welfare would be filled from other sections of the civil service.

My staff, as might be expected, reacted very bitterly to the news. I had recruited these people for a new office, they had worked very hard to establish it and, now, I was letting them down. I assured them that I would get their jobs restored before long but they laughed at my predictions. Nobody, least of all a public servant, ever challenged a government and won.

In the meantime, I rang the Minister for Finance, Ray MacSharry, and suggested to him that surely he was not going to prevent the Office of the Ombudsman from continuing the good work it had embarked upon and which would now be drastically reduced if he went ahead with his cuts. He assured me that he was aware of the good work the Office was doing, but he was under strict orders to effect cutbacks across the board. He regretted what was happening to my office but there was nothing he could do about it. I told him I was sure he could find the missing £100,000 elsewhere – that, as an old friend, I was confident he would not strike such a mortal blow against my office and that I was now leaving down the phone on the understanding that he would not disappoint me.

Some time later, I learned that he had attempted to replace the deleted £100,000 with savings from another department but when he brought the item before cabinet, Haughey spotted the change, asked for an explanation from MacSharry, said, 'That is not what I wanted,' and crossed out the provision.

We continued with our work in the Office, even though our activities were now very curtailed by the reduction of our resources, and complainants had to be informed that there might be considerable delays in dealing with their grievances. In my annual report to the Oireachtas, I explained the difficulties I was experiencing. I also lobbied a number of politicians to seek their help. Alan Dukes, the Fine Gael leader, was most helpful, even to the extent of going to see Haughey, to present my case for a restoration of funds. All my efforts were fruitless and I awaited the next year's budget provisions with considerable trepidation.

The irony of the situation was that the cutbacks being operated here were being matched by similar cutbacks under Margaret Thatcher in the UK, with one notable exception. The British Office of the Ombudsman was untouched; in fact, its budget was increased.

For a second successive year, my office suffered a reduction of £100,000, and I was forced to let another group of five investigators go, leaving me with half my original staff of twenty investigators. Shortly afterwards, Dermot Curran, who had played such a major role in establishing and building up the Office, announced that he was leaving to take up employment outside the public service. He was surprised that I was not more shocked by his decision.

'Dermot,' I said, 'I have had so many blows at this time that one more or less is not going to make much difference.' I was really shocked, however, when I appointed his deputy, Willie Fagan, to succeed him and the Department of Finance refused to sanction his promotion. It was clear to me now that the senior civil servants, anxious to please their political masters, were going to assist as far as they could in destroying the Office of the Ombudsman. I decided to take off the gloves and to fight politicians and civil servants with every resource I could command.

All my efforts at normal lobbying had failed. Even personal letters to Haughey, reminding him of the fact that his legislation had set up the Office and that it was the last resort of poor people who had nowhere else to go fell on deaf ears. No exceptions could be made.

In accordance with the provisions of the Ombudsman Act which required the Ombudsman to inform the Oireachtas if for any reason he was unable to fulfil his duties, I wrote a special report to the Oireachtas, setting out the situation and indicating that any further reduction in the finances would inevitably lead to the closing of the Office.

The report got extensive publicity, accompanied by strong editorial comment criticising Haughey and the Government for their treatment of the Ombudsman's Office. The matter was raised in the Dáil and Haughey accused me of seeking personal publicity. I immediately responded by saying that his remarks were unbecoming of the Taoiseach and that I was merely fulfilling my obligations under the provisions of the Ombudsman's Act.

The debate went on for some time, with support for my case coming from all parts of the country, including many local authorities where the Government party was in the majority. I knew that Haughey was really rattled when he threatened to call a general election unless the agitation stopped. Eventually, like most excitements which have a nine-day span, interest waned and life returned to normal. I had gained no ground and it was clear that Haughey would not yield unless I found some new weapon.

I had a brainwave. I remembered vaguely the terms of the national agreement between the Government and the social partners. A re-reading of the agreement confirmed my belief that all the signatories to the document had committed themselves to doing nothing during the operation of the agreement which would damage the quality of life for the least well off in our society.

145

I showed a copy of the agreement to one of the most active trade unionists on my staff, asking him if he thought the terms of the pact were being honoured in regard to the finances of the Ombudsman's Office, which was the last avenue of appeal for thousands of poor people.

I left it to himself to decide how the matter might be progressed and I was delighted to read a paragraph in the daily papers a few weeks later which said that the Association of Higher Civil Servants had passed a resolution calling on the Irish Congress of Trade Unions to secure the application of the provisions of the national agreement to the financing of the Ombudsman's Office.

I opened my Sunday paper two weeks later to read that the General Secretary of Congress, Peter Cassells, had asked the chairman of the committee responsible for monitoring the progress of the agreement to put on the agenda for the next meeting of the committee, the question of the financing of the Ombudsman's Office. I went into the office the following morning, waving the paper in one hand and assuring the staff that our fight had been won. They did not believe a word of my claim but I told them that I had been around politics too long not to know when victory was in sight. I knew that Haughey would not fight Congress on this one.

My predictions were right and, some weeks later, the Minister for Finance, Ray MacSharry told the Dáil that the Government had agreed to carry out a review of the financing of the Office of the Ombudsman.

A team of civil servants from Finance arrived in my office shortly afterwards to carry out a review. I told them that whatever direction their review might take I would not accept fewer than four teams of investigators (three to a team) and four senior investigators to head up the teams, in addition to an overall Director of the Office. They objected strongly to having conditions laid down but I insisted that my minimum demands represented a *sine qua non*. If they were not conceded, I would carry on my fight in public until I got what the Office needed. I was able to offer the five investigators, who had been let go to the Department of Social Welfare in the first cutback, their old jobs back. Most of them had by this time settled down in their new positions, and only one of the five returned.

⌘　　⌘　　⌘

As the end of my six-year term as Ombudsman approached in1989, I began to think vaguely about the future. I knew that Haughey would seek to replace me, particularly following my confrontation with him over the funding of the Office. He was unaware of my involvement in securing the intervention of the Irish Congress of Trade Unions in the dispute but he probably suspected that it had not happened accidentally.

As I learned later, he had already selected a successor for the Office of Ombudsman. At the same time, I was confident that the Progressive Democrat members of the Government, Des O'Malley and Bobby Molloy, would not agree to my departure. I did not suspect that the decision to get rid of me would be taken without reference to the cabinet, and that the question of the appointment of a new Ombudsman would be considered by only Haughey and his immediate colleagues.

About three months before the end of my term of office, officials of the Department of Finance contacted my office to enquire about the procedures for the filling of the Office. My officers provided the necessary information. In my innocence, I thought that my position might be protected by the fact that Albert Reynolds, the Minister for Finance, who had always been friendly, was aware of the need for a decision to be made on the appointment. I made no approaches to anybody about my reappointment. I had adopted a fatalistic approach to the question – if I was not reappointed, so be it. I would survive.

Shortly after this, I had a conversation with my friend, Joe Fahy, who was in charge of the office of the European Parliament in Dublin. Over coffee in a restaurant off Dawson Street, he asked me if I had received any intimation from the Government about my reappointment. I told him that there had been an enquiry about the procedures from the Department of Finance but that there had been no further contact and I had not lobbied anybody on my behalf.

At that point, Terry Keane came into the café and sat down at a table close by. I switched the conversation from local to European politics, much to Joe Fahy's surprise, since he did not know the lady in question. I had to wait until we got outside to explain my predicament in trying to talk about Haughey with his girlfriend close by.

Some weeks later, Joe had cause to remember our conversation when he was visited in his office in Strasbourg by Barry Desmond, the Labour TD who later became a member of the European Court of Audit. He was accompanied by Fergus Finlay, who was Dick Spring's personal assistant and spokesman. They discussed the general scene back in Dublin, and Barry Desmond asked Joe Fahy if there had been any news of the filling of the post of Ombudsman. Joe repeated to him the contents of his conversation with me in Dublin sometime earlier and said that, so far as he knew, that remained the position.

Barry pointed out that it was now the last week's sitting of the Dáil before the end of my six-year appointment, and that a motion to fill the post should be on the Dáil order paper for the week. He had with him a copy of the order paper and it contained no reference to the Ombudsman. Fergus Finlay rang Dick Spring's office in Dublin to alert his leader to the situation.

Dick Spring went immediately down to the Dáil chamber and asked Haughey what the Government's intentions were in regard to the filling of the post. Haughey replied that the matter was being dealt with in the normal way and that an announcement would be made in due course. Spring said that he was not satisfied with the reply and that he would be returning to the subject.

The following day, which was the last day of the Dáil before the end of my appointment, Spring put down a special notice question and was joined with similar special notice questions by Alan Dukes, the Fine Gael leader, and by Proinsias de Rossa, the leader of the smaller party, Democratic Left.

The Ceann Comhairle, Sean Treacy, was generally very reluctant to permit special notice questions but, on this occasion, he permitted all three questions to be processed. Haughey, reluctant to deal with a matter which he regarded as beneath his attention, passed the questions on to Albert Reynolds, who repeated Haughey's bland answer of the previous day. The matter was being dealt with in the normal way. Words were exchanged but no satisfaction was derived and the matter was left hanging in the air.

The short exchange was, however, carried on the intercom system from the Dáil chamber into the party offices upstairs, where it was heard by the PD leader, Des O'Malley. He waited in the corridor for Haughey as he left the Dáil to return to his office, and asked him for an explanation of what was happening. Haughey made some vague reply about 'backwoodsmen in the party' who were giving him difficulty. O'Malley told him that, whatever his difficulties, the PDs would not tolerate my departure from the Office of Ombudsman. Haughey told him that he would have the matter reviewed and would be back to him as quickly as possible. Within the hour, Haughey rang to say that I was being reappointed for a second term. The announcement was made public in time for the six o'clock news on RTÉ.

I had left the office half an hour earlier, unaware of whether or not I still had a job. I missed the RTÉ news and was almost home when I met my son, Kieran, travelling in his car in the opposite direction. He let down his window to shout 'congratulations'. He had just heard the news on his car radio.

The plot to get rid of me was quite clever, as I worked out later. Had I not been reappointed before the end of my term, I could not have been reappointed at all, since I had passed the age limit of 61 years. Nobody over the age of 61 can be appointed to the Office. The Dáil would have been faced with a motion in the next session to appoint my successor. Excuses would have been made to the effect that, because of an administrative oversight, it had not been realised that certain age qualifications had to be met; that since I had not been reappointed immediately at the end of my first term, the new appointment would have to be regarded as exactly that – a new appointment and not a reappointment. There would be expressions of regret that my valuable services had been lost, but the main objective would have been realised. I would have been disposed of.

It was a clever plot, conceived by senior civil servants with the backing of their political masters and supported by internal legal opinion. However, because of Des O'Malley's intervention, I was back in my office the following week to continue my work as Ombudsman for a further five years, until I reached the statutory age limit of 67 years, in 1994.

⌘　　⌘　　⌘

At the end of 1993, the Office of the Ombudsman completed its first ten years of work.

In that time, a total of 37,122 complaints was received, of which 5,269 were outside jurisdiction. Of the 31,853 complaints examined, 6,705 were resolved in favour of the complainants; assistance was provided in 8,525 cases; and 11,684 complaints were not upheld. A further 4,303 were discontinued or withdrawn.

The first ten years were eventful ones for the Office of the Ombudsman. Ireland was one of the last countries in Europe to establish an institution which had already been functioning in most other European countries for a long number of years. It could be argued that the system of political representation in Ireland, with national and local politicians making representations on behalf of their constituents, was sufficiently effective to avoid any obvious cases of injustice; but it must have become clear to members of the Oireachtas in the 1970s especially, that, with the growth of bureaucracy and with more and more people availing of public services, the risks of serious injustice were increasing. It was also becoming clear to politicians that, without access to the files, their task of trying to unravel the details of complex cases was becoming impossible. The provision in the Ombudsman Act of 1980 to give the Ombudsman authority to obtain all documents immediately and without question was the most powerful weapon in the armoury of the new institution.

The first ten years confirmed my impression of the Irish Public Service as a service of quality and integrity. If mistakes occurred, and they inevitably did in all organisations, public and private, they were mainly the result of overwork, the failure to take all relevant factors into account, or a misinterpretation of the law in particular cases. A complaint of actual ill-will towards a member of the public was very rare.

Despite the hostility of some older members, there was a considerable measure of goodwill from younger public servants generally towards the Office of the Ombudsman in its early days. This goodwill increased with the years, and public servants were very willing to co-operate with the Ombudsman and indeed to promote improvement in the system.

There was, unfortunately, a reluctance by some public servants to co-operate with the Office and, more importantly, to implement recommendations after the Office had carried out formal investigations into particular complaints. It is understandable that senior public servants with long experience in particular areas should find it difficult to come to terms with a new and what they sometimes regarded as an intrusive office. Several confrontations, which left everybody bruised, were undesirable but, at the end of the day, they may have been useful in so far as they made clear to particular public servants that the Office of the Ombudsman would not yield on issues which were seen as fundamental and on which reasonable recommendations had been made.

Battles of the early years were mainly a memory by now, but from time to time major difficulties were still encountered because some public bodies could not accept that they had been guilty of maladministration. Eventually, and only after detailed correspondence and contacts, they were faced with the possibility of a special report being made to the Oireachtas unless they were prepared to respond reasonably to the Ombudsman's recommendation. This provision in the Ombudsman's Act is also a very powerful weapon which has been given to the Office of the Ombudsman. I was very glad that, over the first ten years, despite my being compelled on a number of occasions to inform public bodies and public servants of the possibility of my using this power, I never had occasion to use it. The implementation by public bodies of the recommendations made by the Ombudsman over the first ten years effectively demonstrated the fallacy of the criticism at the time the Office was being set up that it would be 'a mouse that roared'.

The number and the nature of the thousands of complaints received over the years fully illustrated the great need for an independent agency to examine complaints by the public. Many complaints had been festering for years, causing considerable bitterness and frustration. Some of them had been examined at the highest level in the political system but, up to the time the Office of the Ombudsman was established, they had never been subjected to independent scrutiny.

Suddenly, with the power of access to all documents available to the Ombudsman's Office, all justified complaints were capable of being resolved. For people who never had reason to complain about their dealings with the public service, this might appear to be a small thing, but for people who tried for years to obtain what they regarded as their rights, it was a huge development.

The number of complaints rose steadily in the first three years from 1984 until they had reached over 5,000 a year. The Office was barely keeping its head above water at that stage in trying to deal with this flood of complaints when the financial cutbacks hit the Office in 1987. The work of the Office was immediately and seriously affected. It became impossible for the Office to fulfil its statutory obligations and I was obliged under the provisions of the Ombudsman Act to inform the Oireachtas of the position.

Fortunately the situation was rescued, and funds were provided to restore a number of staff to enable the Office to get back on track again. The number of complaints levelled off at approximately 3,000 a year and the existing staff of thirty-three was just sufficient to enable the Office to deal efficiently with this number of complaints.

The resources would be stretched, however, if a large number of formal investigations had to be conducted. Fortunately the vast bulk of complaints were resolved without the need for a formal investigation. Informal contacts with the public bodies concerned and their co-operation and goodwill were sufficient in many cases to bring the matter to a reasonably speedy conclusion.

One of the most encouraging features of the work of the Ombudsman was the willingness of individual government departments and other public bodies to examine anomalies outlined by the Office in reports over the years. Several very important changes in the administration of various schemes were made, with considerable benefit to the members of the public.

The decision of the Oireachtas to extend the remit of the Office in the early years to Bórd Telecom imposed some strain on the resources of the Office because of the influx of the very large number of Telecom complaints. That number fell dramatically in the 1990s following the introduction of itemised billing for telephones. This enabled the Office to deal with the increasing number of complaints in the areas of local authorities and health boards which were brought within remit at the same time as Telecom.

The path was now set firmly for the future. The Office was accepted and recognised by the public as an independent agency which would impartially examine complaints and would take every possible step to have cases of genuine grievance resolved.

For me, personally, those ten years provided a unique opportunity for which I was extremely grateful. It had been a rare privilege to have had the opportunity to work from the foundation with an organisation capable of achieving widespread benefit for people, and to know that the Office had succeeded in resolving thousands of complaints which, in most cases, would never have been resolved without its existence.

OFFICE OF THE OMBUDSMAN, 1984–1993

In the Report of the All-Party Committee on Administrative Justice (May 1977), which recommended the establishment of the Office of the Ombudsman, it was anticipated that: 'The Ombudsman, in the discharge of his functions, will bring to the attention of the Oireachtas those areas in which the rights of the citizen could be safeguarded either by improved appellate procedure or, perhaps less expensively, by the amendment of over-complicated legislation.'

In the course of the first ten years and the receipt of just over 37,000 complaints, I had occasion, in my annual reports, to refer to the type of situations envisaged in the All-Party Report. As a result of these references, several important changes occurred in our legislative and administrative system.

In a number of these cases, the Office was not alone in raising the issues: the views of the Office were part of the general concern expressed by a number of interested parties in the need for improvements in the system. Some of the more significant changes included:

Old Age Pensions

One of the first, and the most worrying, series of complaints to my Office from 1984 onwards related to the unfairness which many older people experienced in the system of 'averaging' of social insurance stamps and which precluded an estimated 2,000 people, aged 66 or over, from obtaining Contributory Old Age Pension because they did not meet the required minimum 'average' of twenty contributions per year. This anomaly was removed for many of them by the introduction, by the Department of Social Welfare, of pro-rata pensions for persons who have an average of five contributions upwards and who came back into full insurance in 1974. The improvement was very welcome but I still continued to receive complaints from a number of older people who were unaffected by the change because they did not meet the requirement of coming back into full insurance in 1974.

Compensation for Late Payments

An issue which led to serious difficulty, before it was eventually resolved, was the question of restoration of the true value of money to persons who had been incorrectly refused benefits by the Department of Social Welfare over lengthy periods. The practice was to pay the arrears of benefit at the rate provided for in the legislation of the particular year. My office contended that account should be taken of inflation in the interim. The issue was eventually resolved as I was preparing to submit a special report to the Oireachtas indicating the unfairness of paying people benefits to which they were legally entitled at a rate which took no account of the decline in the value of money since the original failure to pay arose.

Discrimination against Husbands and Widowers
I drew attention in my annual reports of 1984 and 1986 to the unfair way in which widowers and deserted husbands were treated by the state in so far as they were entitled to claim much less state assistance then would their wives in similar circumstances. This appeared to me to represent a distinct discrimination against men. Changes in social welfare legislation brought a considerable improvement in this area in so far as men now qualify for the Lone Parent Allowance and would shortly be eligible for a Contributory Widower's Pension.

Dependent Domicile
In 1984, I drew attention also to the unfairness of the concept of dependent domicile, under which a wife could be deprived of certain benefits because she was regarded as having the same domicile as her husband, even though he might have deserted her and have been living abroad for a number of years while she continued to reside in Ireland. The concept of dependent domicile was abolished in 1986.

Free Electricity Allowance
I drew attention to the fact that people who use night-rate electricity do not have the night-rate units used taken into account for the purposes of the Free Electricity Allowance administered by the Department of Social Welfare. I explained that this can be inequitable in the case of people whose usage of standard-rate electricity is not sufficient to use up their full allowance of free units. I was very pleased with the announcement by the Minister for Social Welfare that he intended to deal with this anomaly in the near future, thus ensuring that people who use night-rate electricity would have the same actual benefit from the allowance as do all other beneficiaries.

Disabled Person's Maintenance Allowance Payments (DPMA)
My staff found that people who applied for the payment of
DPMA were being paid by some health boards only from the
date of approval of their application. I pointed out to these boards
that their procedure was not in accordance with the law and that
applicants for DPMA who were found eligible were entitled to
payment from the date of receipt of their applications. The
Department of Health accepted that this was the correct
interpretation of the law and new procedures were brought into
operation.

Income Assessment for DPMA
In my annual report of 1988, I gave details of various problems in
relation to income assessment for DPMA entitlement, which had
been brought to my notice. I suggested that there was need for
considerable improvement in the legislation governing this area.
I was happy to note that, since then, legislation had been enacted
in respect of two of these problems.

(1) The Disabled Person's (Maintenance Allowance)
Regulations of 1991 and 1992 clarified the position in regard
to the assessment of income where the disabled person's
spouse is in receipt of a payment from the Department of
Social Welfare. Prior to this, health boards did not regard a
person as eligible for DPMA where the spouse was in receipt
of a social welfare payment with which an adult dependant
allowance might be payable. Under the new legislation,
health boards could no longer consider a person in these
circumstances as automatically excluded from entitlement to
DPMA.

(2) The Social Welfare Act, 1990, Section 38, provided for the
recoupment of Supplementary Welfare Allowance from
arrears of DPMA where a person had been receiving
Supplementary Welfare Allowance while awaiting payment of
DPMA. Prior to this, health boards had no statutory basis for

such recoupment as the Overlapping Benefits Regulations, which govern such recoupment from other payments, did not include DPMA. When DPMA was awarded, it was usual for health boards to reduce the amount of arrears due by the amount of Supplementary Welfare Allowance already paid.

Lack of Provision for Adoptive Mothers
In my annual report for 1990, I drew attention to the lack of provision for adoptive mothers in the area of leave from work, social welfare payments and social insurance credits. These issues arose from a particular complaint I received in 1990. I was not able to uphold the particular complaint as the bodies concerned had acted correctly within the existing law. However, I suggested in my report that consideration should be given to the statutory provision of adoption leave and adoption benefit (including the granting of social insurance credits) in the case of adoptive mothers.

In his 1992 budget statement, the Minister for Finance announced that the Government:

> will be promoting legislation to provide for leave from employment for adoptive mothers and intend making available a benefit to these mothers along the lines of the existing maternity benefit scheme for women in employment. These new arrangements will operate for 10 weeks immediately following the placing of the child with the adoptive parents and will be introduced later this year.

Public Service Widows
I was surprised to discover that some widows of former civil servants were unaware of their rights to claim social welfare pensions on the death of their husbands and that some departments did not automatically inform them of this right. One widow had failed to claim her pension for fourteen years

because she was unaware of her rights. It was agreed that in future all departments of state would inform widows of former civil servants of their rights in this regard.

Antiquated Law

In my 1993 annual report, I referred to complaints I had received from householders in the County Dublin area about the fact that they had to pay for the repair of leaks to water supply pipes between the water main and the stopcock outside their houses.

The householders in question made the point that they had no control over such pipes which were usually under the public road, and, furthermore, that such leaks were probably caused by the level of traffic on the road. They could not understand how they could be held liable for something that was completely outside their control and, indeed, outside the boundary of their property. In the former Dublin County Council area, the local authority did not have responsibility for these pipes. In addition, Dublin Corporation, which was responsible for the supply of water in certain areas of South County Dublin, the so-called Extra Municipal Area, was also not empowered to accept liability for the service pipes in that area.

Dublin Corporation and the former Dublin County Council argued that, in the absence of legislation that would allow them to accept responsibility for water service pipes, the law as it stood placed responsibility for repairs to such pipes on the householders in these areas. The relevant legislation was the Dublin Corporation Waterworks Act, 1861, and the Local Government (Dublin) Act, 1930, under which Dublin Corporation accepted responsibility, within the borough area of Dublin only, for maintaining water service pipes up to a point 9 inches from a consumer's property.

When I first received complaints on this matter in 1984, I carried out a detailed examination of the relevant legislative provisions and I discussed them with the Department of the

Environment. The response, at the time, was that the question of changing the law in this area was being considered in the context of legislation relating to the reorganisation of local government.

Following a further approach, the Department reported to me that these anomalies would be taken into account in the preparation of new legislation arising (a) from commitments in relation to local government reform contained in the Programme for Partnership Government and (b) from the creation of new local authority structures in the greater Dublin area.

I was happy to report that the Local Government (Dublin) Act, 1993, gave the three new Dublin local authorities (Fingal, Dún Laoghaire-Rathdown and South Dublin County Council) the power to maintain branch pipes from the water main to the curtilage of any premises.

By resolutions in January 1994, in the course of the passing of their estimates, the three authorities agreed to accept responsibility for such maintenance.

I must also mention a number of areas where complaints continued to arise and for which no solution had yet been achieved when I left office.

DPMA Income Test

I drew attention on a number of occasions to a serious anomaly in the application of the income test for DPMA in the case of a married person whose spouse is in employment. The approach being adopted was harsh by comparison with the approach adopted in the case of other means-tested payments, such as Unemployment Assistance. In the case of DPMA, the general practice of the health boards is to have regard to the gross income of the working spouse, with no allowance being made for the normal statutory deductions (e.g. PRSI and PAYE Income Tax) or for necessary work-related expenses. As a result of this approach, some couples affected by the practice are forced to live on an income which may not even be equal to that of a couple totally dependent on DPMA. In the case of Unemployment Assistance, for example, where the applicant's spouse is in employment, the Department of Social Welfare makes allowances for PRSI and income tax deductions, and for expenses necessarily incurred in the course of the employment. I could see no reason why the health boards would not take a similar approach in relation to a DPMA applicant whose spouse is in employment.

Rent Allowance for Local Authority Tenants
Another issue, to which I drew attention on a number of occasions, related to the entitlement of local authority tenants to be paid a rent allowance under the Supplementary Welfare Allowance (SWA) scheme. Some local authority tenants paid rent at a level which, if it were being paid to a private landlord, would attract a rent allowance under the SWA scheme. However, health boards, acting on the advice of the Department of Social Welfare, generally refused to pay rent allowance in such cases, even though the consequence was that the applicants were left with a post-rent income which was, in some cases, significantly less than that guaranteed under the SWA scheme. I pointed out that people caught in this trap were being refused the additional assistance solely because they were renting from a local authority rather than from a private landlord. At the time of my last annual report, the Department of Social Welfare and the Department of the Environment were in ongoing discussions in an attempt to resolve this problem.

Anomalies Relating to Separated Persons
In my annual reports for 1991 and 1992, I drew attention to anomalies in relation to the different treatments afforded by the Revenue Commissioners and by the Department of Social Welfare to persons who were living with, but who were not married to, each other.

Since the Revenue Commissioners and the Department of Social Welfare were acting in accordance with legislation, I could not uphold these complaints. I considered that these were matters for the Oireachtas and the alleviation of the obvious adverse effect was not within the competence of my office.

Assessment of Benefit and Privilege

Over my ten years in the Office, one of the most consistent areas of complaint related to the assessment of benefit and privilege in the case of Unemployment Assistance applicants. While acknowledging that the difficulties arising here have been mitigated to some extent over the years, it seems to me that there is still a serious problem to be resolved. Where an applicant for Unemployment Assistance is living with other people, and where those other people (typically parents) have income, the effect of the benefit and privilege assessment is to allocate some of the household income to the applicant. This has the effect of reducing the rate of Unemployment Assistance payable. I suggested that, whatever the merits of assessing benefit and privilege in the case of younger people living at home with their parents, it might not be appropriate to assess it in the case of people over 25 years of age, particularly where the applicant was financially independent prior to becoming unemployed.

My second term as Ombudsman was much less stressful than my first. Looking back over the early years, it seemed to me that we had been living in a constant nightmare, with senior civil servants watching expectantly for us to fall on our face, and many politicians, particularly at local level, watching for an opportunity to slap us down. When I was invited in those early years to address a conference of local authority representatives on the working of the Office, many of them openly read their newspapers while I delivered my lecture, showing their contempt for the Office.

As time passed, however, and the hostile councillors began to see many of their colleagues getting assistance from my office for their constituents, they began to realise that the Ombudsman's Office might be a useful adjunct to their efforts. Senior civil servants also started to change their attitudes and some even became quite helpful. My belief in the future, however, rested with the younger breed of civil servants who were much more open and much more willing to try out new ideas.

A general air of acceptance for the new office began to manifest itself, but at the back of my mind at all times was the fear that if Haughey got into power, the Office would suffer. In 1986, of course, the chop came and, for the next two years, I had to fight a desperate battle, with all the odds stacked against me. However, I knew that if I lost the fight, one of the most enlightened defences of democracy ever set up in this country would be destroyed. Many people, including higher civil servants, were unable to understand my determination not to let the Office be wiped out. I heard that they were questioning among themselves why the Ombudsman's Office should get special treatment when every other department was suffering.

My response to that argument was that the alleged purpose of the cutbacks was to save money, but no money was being saved by reducing the staff in my office – these people were simply being transferred to other departments who had to pay their salaries. But logic had no place in the scheme of things. Haughey was in charge and his edict had to be obeyed.

One minister I was aware was on my side during all the difficulties, without declaring his hand publicly, was Bertie Ahern, who, I was informed by a friend in the civil service, had gone to Haughey and offered to lend staff from his Department of Labour to my office to enable us to continue our work. I was told that Haughey rudely rejected the proposal.

A second minister, Michael Smith, came to me to urge me to keep the heart up – that things would eventually change. I was grateful to both these men for their support at a time when I was really close to despair and there appeared to be no way back.

Fortunately, I was able to get the trade unions on board, and the Office of the Ombudsman was saved. Equally important, I knew that the Office could never again be threatened. This assurance was a great comfort from 1988 onwards, so that for the last six years of my time in the Office of the Ombudsman, I could go about my work without looking over my shoulder at the politicians.

On 31 October 1994, I closed the door of my office for the last time, conscious of the atmosphere of fear and trepidation with which I had first entered the office on 1 January 1984, little knowing that my worst fears would be confirmed and that the reality of the first five years would be a constant nightmare. But it was a challenge and a rare privilege to be associated with the start-up of a new institution, which was capable of achieving so much. I would not have missed that opportunity for anything.

Appendix

Chronology of Events of the Arms Crisis

1969

12 August	Apprentice Boys' Parade in Derry; battle of Bogside begins.
13 August	Violence in Derry continues; barricades go up in Belfast; Jack Lynch goes on television to say that Irish Government will not stand by.
14 August	British troops arrive in Derry; violence breaks out in Belfast with four people shot dead.
15 August	Violence continues in Belfast where British troops arrive.
16 August	Sniping continues in Belfast. Government sets up fund for the relief of distress in Northern Ireland, under the control of C. J. Haughey, who is also made responsible, with Jim Gibbons, for building up the Irish Army to be ready to deal with an emergency situation. The decision to set aside £100,000 for the relief of distress in Northern Ireland is taken but the money is not approved by the Dáil until 18 March 1970.
3 October	Training of Derry citizens in Irish Army camp at

	Fort Dunree, County Donegal, stopped on instructions of Taoiseach. On the same day, Captain James Kelly goes to Kinsealy to tell Haughey of a proposed meeting in Bailieboro the following day. Haughey gives him £500 for expenses and tells him that £50,000 is available for the purchase of guns.
4 October	Meeting at Bailieboro, County Cavan, of representatives of Northern Ireland defence committees. Captain Jim Kelly allegedly informs an attendance of fifteen representatives that a sum of £50,000 is available from Irish Government sources for the purchase of weapons. Kelly later describes this meeting as the genesis of the plan to import arms.
9 October	Account for £5,000 opened by Red Cross in Bank of Ireland, Clones.
16 October	Gardaí brief Berry on Bailieboro meeting. The briefing takes place at Mount Carmel Hospital where Berry has had an emergency operation.
October	Jock Haughey (brother of Charlie) and John Kelly go to London to meet Captain Randall to import arms. Some arms come in.
December	John Kelly and Sean Keenan go to America to meet Liam Kelly about bringing in arms.

1970

January	The IRA splits into the Provisionals and the Officials, following a walk-out from an IRA convention by a group of hardliners led by Ruairí Ó Brádaigh and Seán Mac Stiofáin.
6 February	Army directive on contingency plan issued by Jim Gibbons to Michael Hefferon.
14 February	James Kelly claims that on this day he discussed

	the entire operation with C. J. Haughey, who knew all about it.
4 March	Jim Gibbons learns from Hefferon that Captain Kelly is going to Germany to vet guns for purchase.
25 March	Kelly tells Gibbons of failure to import guns through Dublin Port from Antwerp on City of Dublin but informs him that another attempt is to be made by shipping the guns from Trieste.
Early April	Attempt to bring in guns by air from Vienna thwarted by 'ring of steel' at Dublin Airport.
Early April	Ballymurphy under attack; Blaney calls on Gibbons to enact contingency plan as set down in 6 February directive. Lynch countermands the order.
April 13	Berry claims he told Lynch on this date of the arms plot and of the involvement of Haughey and Blaney. Lynch always claimed that his first knowledge of the operation came on 20 April.
20 April	Berry presents Lynch with a report on the attempted import of guns. Lynch asks him to carry out a full investigation and report back to him the following day.
21 April	Budget Day in Dáil. Haughey is injured in fall from horse and Lynch takes on task of presenting the Budget. Lynch outlines the position to political journalists at Leinster House and appears to one journalist to be curiously unconcerned when asked about the seriousness of Haughey's injuries.
1 May	Captain Kelly retires from Irish Army and is arrested but released the following day.
4 May	Micheál Ó Moráin, the Minister for Justice, resigns after being requested to do so by Jack Lynch.

6 May	C. J. Haughey and Neil Blaney are sacked from Government; Kevin Boland and Junior Minister Paudge Brennan resign in protest; Jack Lynch tells Dáil that he has received information connecting the sacked ministers with a plot to bring in arms illegally. Lynch's move against the sacked ministers follows a visit to him by the leader of Fine Gael, Liam Cosgrave, the previous day. Cosgrave had with him a letter on Garda notepaper, linking the two sacked ministers, as well as Minister Jim Gibbons, Colonel Michael Hefferon and Captain Jim Kelly to the plot.
8 May	Marathon 36-hour debate begins in Dáil which continues until 10 p.m. on 9 May.
27 May	Jim Kelly, John Kelly and Albert Luykx arrested on arms conspiracy charges.
28 May	Haughey and Blaney arrested on similar charges.
2 July	Information refused against Blaney; others returned for trial.
22 September	Arms Trial opens in the Four Courts before Judge Andreas O'Keefe
29 Setember	Trial stopped and jury discharged after row between judge and defence counsel Ernest Wood.
6 October	New trial opens before Judge Henchy.
23 October	The four defendants are acquitted.

Index